Courageous World Catalysts

36 Inspirational Stories by Changemakers on their Missions for Global Impact

This anthology project was led and compiled by Vickie Gould, Law of Attraction Business and Book Coach. www.vickiegould.com email vickie@vickiegould.com

Cover by: Michael Corvin
Edited by: Andrea McCurry

Co-authored by

- Vickie Gould, Law of Attraction Business and Book Coach
- Carri Adcock, Speaker, Break-though and Transformational Coach
- Briana Baptiste, Entrepreneur, Language Enthusiast, Kibun Goddess
- Michael Barnes, Business Success and Leadership Coach
- Brenda Benalcazar, Licensed Wealth Coach with Elite Hathaway, Author and Speaker
- Shauna-Kaye L. Brown, Motivational Speaker and Empowerment Coach
- Anya Connolly, M.S., Transformational Life and Wellness Coach
- Karin Anne Davis, CTDP, Creativity & Innovation Specialist
- Elizabeth de Moraes, Certified Personal Branding and Video Visibility Success Coach
- Sanura X. Dean, Empowerment Coach and Speaker
- Dorothy-Inez Del Tufo, Confidence and Personal Presence Coach
- Charles Dray, C.Ht., Clinical Hypnotherapist and NLP Life Coach
- Alicia Ford, Mindset Strategist and Client Attraction Mentor
- Justina Ford, Christian Mindset and Soul-Alignment Strategist
- Jennifer Gardner, Christian NLP Life Coach & Hypnotherapist
- Brooks Gibbs, Powerful, Passionate Mirror (Mentor and Coach)
- Debbie Hart, Life and Relationship Coach, Victim to Victor
- Adaku L. Ikotun, Inspirational & Motivational Coach, Founder of Adaku Inspires
- Mofoluwaso Ilevbare, Author, Speaker, The 'Unstoppable Life' Coach.
- Kierra Jones, Expertise Empowerment Coach and Shine Strategist, Author & Speaker
- Delia Joseph, CPC Improveologist
- Sharon Kambale, Holistic Guru, Change Agent, Business and Marketing Strategist
- Dawn Laveck-Palfi, Self-Love and Self-Care Advocate/Coach

- Kim Maksym, The Fairy Best DogMother, Holistic Nutritionist, Energy Therapist, Wellness Intuitive for Animals & People
- Melinda Maxwell-Smith, MT, RCST, SEP, Bodyworker
- Janis Melillo, Wellness/Transformation Health Coach, International Best Selling Co-Author
- Trudy Miller, Architect, Fashion Designer, Body Image Expert
- Maxine Nwaneri, Success Coach & Founder of The Future is Greater
- Jane Richardson, PhD Communication Consultant, Expert Witness & Author
- Kanelli Scalcoyannis, Success Coach & Founder of Luscious Life
- Sherrod Schuler, MBA Minister, Motivational Speaker and Financial Wellness Coach
- Simran- Transformational Coach, Soul Mentor, Energy Medicine Practitioner, Author
- Shaneil Stewart, #1 International Bestselling Author, Coach, Speaker, Entrepreneur and Philanthropist
- Johanna Stock, Wealth Executive, Public Speaker, Mentor
- Tiki Tikifaces Tunstall, Minister and CEO of TIKIFACES
- Fan Zhang, M.A.Sc. Health Coach and Nu Skin Business Coach

Do you dream of one day becoming a published author? Do you want to make your mark and have a lasting impact? Do you know that there are people out there waiting on your message?

Then, **I'd like to invite you to participate in the next anthology** and become a Best Seller like the authors in this anthology.

All you have to do is turn in your story and I'm going to give you easy-to-follow steps to writing it so that it speaks to those people who need your help. I'm also going to take away the tech overwhelm by publishing the book for you and guaranteeing the Best Seller status. Plus, I'm even going to have your story edited by my team.

Go here for details on the next project – join or get on the waiting list: http://bit.ly/nextanthology

Acknowledgement

Thank you to all the amazing authors in this book and your courage to share your stories. I am truly humbled to compile this book together with your help in order to fulfill our collective mission for global impact.

Special thanks to Andrea McCurry for her fabulous job editing everyone's stories. This could not have been created without your huge support!

Table of Contents

Dedication

This book is dedicated to our readers. It is for you that we compiled these stories. Our hearts are open for you. It's our hope that you will be inspired to see yourself in our stories and know that you too can overcome just as we have.

If you have ever thought you couldn't be or do something in life or that you had to conform to the world and fit in to be happy, this book will show you how to find your own source of happiness.

If you've ever wanted to pursue your passion as your own boss by being an entrepreneur, but thought you weren't enough or plain couldn't, this book will show you how anything is possible when you step up to your calling.

If you've ever wondered why you had to go through adversity, let this book help you see the gift in your struggles.

If you'd like to hear how other people, just like you, came to do what they do - if you'd like to know how following their passions has filled their soul AND how you can do it too, this book will prove to you that whatever life throws at you or how you were raised to think about who you could be or what you could or couldn't do, let this book prove to you that you can choose to turn adversity into advantage and devastation into victory.

We hope you'll be inspired to GO FOR YOUR DREAMS, FIND YOUR PURPOSE AND RESPOND TO YOUR CALLING by living life fully as YOU.

Introduction

The idea of an anthology had been on my mind for some time. I knew that a compilation of stories from inspiring leaders would have a great positive impact on the world. When I put the idea out to my network, I was excited with the quality of people whom this project attracted. What I didn't fully imagine was the power that would be within 36 heart-felt stories all told together. This is now what we present to you.

Each and every co-author in this anthology is an overcomer. Each also has a very personal story to share and a message to leave behind. We knew that it was part of our duty and calling to share what we had been through, how we got to where we are and why we do what we do.

In the process of reading through the anthology, we hope that you will be inspired to see yourself in these stories and relate them to your own life for inspiration and to create positive change.

You can read the book in any order that you'd like. You can pick the titles that speak the loudest to you or you can just go in order.

Find that story that speaks to you and if you'd like, reach out to the author to find out how they can further help you.

Everyone in this world has a story to share and these are our journeys.

The Girl in the Mirror
By Vickie Gould

The person staring back at me in the bathroom mirror was one I barely recognized. I could barely stand. The fight was gone. The sparkle in the eye was gone. There were a few more pounds all over, and the face – it was droopy. I looked OLD. When did I turn into this person? Who was I anymore?

Years had passed by and my children barely knew me. All they knew was that mom was sick and she didn't go to their stuff. No school parties. No field trips. Going to a performance or sporting event meant I would be wiped out for almost a full week afterwards.

And my husband? I don't even want to go there. He suffered while I was bitter and angry that I had a reluctant caregiver.

I hate to admit the thoughts that went through my head as hope flickered away.

"Vickie, you're a drain on the family finances."
"Everyone else would be better off without you."
"You're not useful for anything."
"You're worthless if you can't contribute."

I couldn't even do the laundry anymore. It took too much energy.

I couldn't finish making meals. I'd have to go lie down before I was done.

I couldn't clean the bathroom all at once, so the house was never clean.

I couldn't stay awake for a full day.

What kind of life would this be for the next … 40 or 50 years? What kind of contribution would I make? What kinds of therapy would my children have to go through later? What would they know or remember of me?

I told myself to throw in the towel. End it. Make it quick. But then who would find me? What would happen then? That was too much trauma for my children. Besides, I wanted to meet my one-day grandchildren – I could see their little smiling faces, and I still had a little speck of hope left inside me.

I decided, because it had to be a *decision*, that it was my soul's journey to live. I didn't know how and I didn't know why I was meant to go through this illness. But I did know my time was not up.

As more days turned into more years, I threw everything at Lyme Disease (It was first misdiagnosed as Lupus). It made me even sicker to go through the treatment – it was a get-worse-before-you-get-better type of thing. I tried everything I found that might help, except the pharma, which equaled out-of-pocket expenses. $20k went by in a flash and I wavered back and forth about if it was truly worth it to treat the disease, or if I should just endure a long, drawn out death. Yes, people die from Lyme disease. My friends had been hospitalized, bedridden, and taken from this world. All due to small spirochete bacteria.

It felt like no one believed me. I looked great they all thought. Invisible illnesses are just that – invisible. No one came to help me. I watched other people with cancer get help from the church. I got one meal in four years, and no one offered to take my children for me. But part of that was my fault. I was superwoman in hiding. I didn't want to admit that I needed help. I was strong. I was tough. And it was exhausting.

Bitter. I was growing old and bitter. What was I supposed to do with this life?

And so the search began for the reason for my illness. Some days I would lie in bed and watch Netflix, thinking of nothing, and other days I would investigate what I was supposed to be learning from all of it. Obviously, God thought I was some tough cookie if this was what I was meant to go through.

I started to investigate my heart and I looked back on the previous 40 years of my life, trying to find the message in it all.

All I found was regrets. Regrets from putting myself last, squelching my voice, letting everyone else go first, and telling myself that what I wanted didn't matter. It became more and more evident that I had never really lived.

I had lived a fake life those 40 years.

It looked really good on the outside. I had received a good education just like my mom had wanted me to. Climbed the corporate ladder, married, had kids, and had a husband that one of my friends said, "adores you."

Yet in reality, I knew there was always something missing. That's why every two years in corporate, I had to quit and jump careers. I got a great raise and felt accomplished. I got the corner office with the double-sided windows, but what I was really looking for was a new high, a new challenge, and that exciting piece because something was missing.

And nothing filled that void. I always had to have a side gig going on to fuel my creativity and passion. But in that case too, I jumped from thing to thing like a restless animal. Need I say "caged?"

Upon reflection, I came to realize that I had never lived the life I was truly born for, and my illness was my detour to get back on track. I'd always asked God to hit me with a two-by-four instead of being subtle, and I guess I got exactly what I asked for.

Thus commenced the many times I spent crying in the pitch black dark of night next to my sleeping husband, or on the cold bathroom floor. Sometimes I'd sob and sometimes I'd try to muffle it so that I didn't wake him up.

I lamented the days and years that I had lost. I regretted all those times I told myself no. I regretted the times I had squelched my intuition as "silly" or "unfounded" and let my head and logic rule my choices. And I vowed no more. If and when I got better, I would actually show up to the life I was given.

So as I threw more and more things at Lyme Disease, I did get progressively better. I was strict with myself and adamant that I was going to overcome, and it was this intention that kept me going.

I remember the plateaus of healing and I also recalled the day I asked myself if my feeling better was going to "stick." I was scared to think that perhaps the worst was over and I was on the other side. Other times, I felt better, but then it would get bad again, which is typical of the cycle of ups and downs with flares from Lyme.

But this day it was different. I was tentatively cautious with my thoughts. "Don't jinx it, Vickie," I said to myself. It'd been a few months where I felt pretty human and functional. Was this the end of Lyme? Was it time to celebrate that it was over?

And so it was.

My turn had come around again.

"No regrets," I reminded myself. "No regrets."

I thought back on my childhood days. I was always the smiley one. I had a glimmer in my eye – not the mischievous kind, but the star struck kind. I once dreamt of being famous, walking on the red carpet, being on TV, writing a book … having people recognize my face. I wanted my name written in history. I wanted impact and legacy.

I didn't know how, but I knew that's what was going to happen because I was no longer going to stay quiet, hidden, and small. I would be the ME that God created me to be.

Part of this new calling in my life was to write a book so that's what I did. What I didn't realize would happen was that by sharing my story, it inspired others to grab onto that hope that they could get well too. They understood that there was meaning in the pain and a message for them also.

They started to come to me, one by one, asking how I got better.

And after those people passed through my life, the next ones asked how I got my story out, how I wrote my books.

I realized pretty quickly that my journey through illness was so that I could urge others to not waste their time. They too could make an impact and leave their mark here on earth before they're gone. No regrets. Time is always of the essence.

We are not promised one more day and we have a duty to fulfill our life's calling and purpose, not to squelch who we are or try to conform to what the world expects from us.

The girl I see in the mirror now has the sparkle back in her eye. She's now known for the statement heels that she couldn't balance in with Lyme, and she wears them as a symbol that she's kicked illness and taken her life back.

Oh, and she's back to being that smiley one too; she just plain enjoys LIVING.

I guess the rest is "history," now that I've figured out that my purpose is to help others to leave their legacy and in doing so, I leave mine.

Vickie Gould is a certified Law of Attraction Business and Book Coach. She helps her clients go from blank page to Best Seller and beyond. As a result of working with her, Vickie's clients are able to help others struggling like they once did, attract ideal clients, make the impact that they want and leave a lasting legacy through their Best-Selling Books.

She has been seen on ABC, NBC, CBS and Fox. She often contributes to HuffPost and Thrive Global, both started by Arianna Huffington. She also previously published the online magazine, Real Deal Magazine.

Vickie has four Best-Selling books of her own and she has been involved and mentioned in numerous of her clients Best-Selling books as well. Her greatest joy is in seeing their message come alive in WORDS. Visit her at www.vickiegould.com

She lives with her husband and three kids in Michigan, along with her addiction to superhero shows on Netflix.

Join her Facebook Group, Real Deal Entrepreneurs at: www.facebook.com/groups/betherealdeal

Follow her on Instagram @ vickiegould

Want to find out if you're a Right or Left Brained writer and how to use those strengths to become an author? Go to bit.ly/freewriterguide to take a quiz and find out, then get your Free Guide.

If There's a Dream in Your Heart, Take Action!
By Mofoluwaso Ilevbare

For God has not given us a spirit of fear but of power,
love, and a sound mind.
~ 2 Tim 1:7 (KJV)

Beep—beeeeeeeep…I jumped up from my cozy bed as soon as I heard the sound from my bedside alarm. This was a very important day and I couldn't afford to be late. My company in Nigeria had just closed a fabulous business year, and this day we were having the grand dinner celebration and awards ceremony for all employees; our own *Grammys.* I looked down at my to-do list:

Confirm the attendees…check!

Confirm the hotel accommodations…check!

Inspect the five shuttle cars…check!

Brief the security men on the protocols…check!

Leave the premises in capable hands…almost check!

Finally, it was time to leave for the celebration. I rushed into the ladies' room to get dressed. My husband had just bought a lovely mint-green trouser suit from Argos for me, and I couldn't wait to launch it on this special night. I had my hair-do, woven with African braids, all tucked in the middle into a style we call "suku." I checked my list of dignitaries as the cars left the premises one after the other, in a convoy escorted by heavy security. I wrapped up everything else and hopped into the last car. Finally, I could get some rest on my two-hour drive to the venue.

Fast forward, twenty minutes later. Bang! Bang! The moment I heard the car screech and come to a halt, I knew something was wrong. The next thing I experienced was the driver slamming the car into reverse mode, at such a speed as though we were on the set of the next sequel to *Fast & Furious.* As I heard more gun shots, I stiffened. I could feel my heart pounding like it would literally burst out of its cage. I could feel the goose pimples all over me, a cold, tingling feeling ran down my spine and my fingers trembled with fear. Then suddenly, the car stopped abruptly, after hitting the headlights of the car behind us. The next thing I remember was seeing my driver abandon the car, bare-footed and running away.

"What just happened? Wake up! Wake up!" I said to myself. "It's only a dream." But no matter how hard I tried to pinch myself, the terrifying sounds of the gun shots kept me in the reality of my situation. I raised my head slightly and looked around. The car was jammed in the middle of several other cars on the highway, most of them already abandoned by their owners. People ran helter-skelter.

"Somebody wake me up. This can't be happening. Not today, not now, not to me!" I whispered over and over again. The pair of brown leather sandals lying at the foot of the pedals in the driver's seat reminded me that only a few seconds earlier, I had a driver. Where was he, and why would he leave me here despite the security training and briefing he had been given time and time again? All I could mutter was, *"Though I walk through the valley of the shadow of death I shall fear no evil...,"* a verse from Psalm 23 in the Bible.

The gunshots became louder and I knew they were coming closer. Armed men, about five of them, with black masks on their faces, big guns in their hands. I watched in dismay as two of them then dragged a middle-aged man and his wife, both of them gorgeously dressed, obviously going for a ceremonial event like me, out of their car, shouting at them. Then I realized that in less than ten minutes, this could be happening to me. Should I stay and raise my hands in surrender? Should I try to run for my dear life? If I stayed, what would be the worst that could happen? If I ran, what would be the worst that could happen?

I mustered a quick prayer "God help me. Give me strength; tell me what to do." Almost immediately, I heard his reply "RUN!" I suddenly felt courage well up inside me and into my legs, so I opened the door to my side slightly, and rolled out onto the highway. I bent my head for fear of stray bullets, and maneuvered in between the jam-packed cars behind me. I raised my head to see where I was heading, just in time to hear one of the armed robbers shout, "Hey you, Stop!"

My legs must have sped like lightning even before my brain processed the words. I scaled a big ditch and crossed the highway to the other side of the road. Gun shots behind me, I felt one fly past me, putting a hole in my loose jacket. Only haziness was in front of me, but all I did was run. Landing on the other side of the road, I ran into the thick forest. The soles of my feet hurt, but I would not stop; the thorns tore at my skin, but I would not stop. By now my Argos mint green trouser suit was no longer a suit, it looked more like a rag. All I kept muttering was, "*Though I walk through the valley of the shadow of death, I will fear no evil*. This is not the day, not here, not now, not me."

I don't know how far I ran, but it may qualify as a half marathon. I slowed down and listened again, still hearing some footsteps, and in the distance, gunshot sounds. Then all of a sudden, my legs weakened under me. I felt no more strength to go on, and I fell to the ground with the last breath in me, landing on an abandoned ant hill in the middle of the forest.

I closed my eyes and muttered over and over again, under my breath *"Though I walk through the valley of the shadow of death, I will fear no evil."*

The seconds passed into minutes and hours, but finally the sun went down. As I listened intently, the footsteps were gone and sounds of gun shots were no more. I had survived, and it was time to find my way back home.

I moved on with life after this nasty experience. It took me weeks to fling away the *blanket of fear* life handed to me that fateful day, but little did I know that three years down the road, I would find myself in another similar near-death experience. My car was hijacked, but this time there was nowhere to run. I stood there in the dark, with a colleague from work, helpless, surrounded by four armed, hungry-looking teenagers with guns pointed to our faces as they struggled to seize the new official car I had been given at work. "Shall we kill her?" one of them asked. "No, let's take her with us." another replied. "Why take her with us? Let's kill her!" another shouted. "Let's just dump her in that ditch." the fourth replied. As I watched them debate my fate, swirling their guns in my face, deep down I knew God was at work YET AGAIN. They concluded to take the car and leave us alone. As I watched them drive off, I whispered with gratitude in my heart "*Though I walk through the valley of the shadow of death, I will fear no evil.*"

Maybe your journey through life has been one of joy, peace, and a family that adores you. Maybe it's been a jungle of emotional roller-coasters and disappointments. I pray you never experience an inch of what I have been through, but why wait until something bad happens to jolt you back into making life matter? These near-death experiences have only strengthened me to become the Best-Selling Author, Speaker, Philanthropist, and Unstoppable Life Strategist that I am today, helping many throughout the globe to kick-start their dreams and be unstoppable at work and life.

So, let me ask, "*Are you satisfied with the life you're living today?*" "*If you could step it up to another level, what should you do differently?*"

What's your DREAM?

Is it to:
- [ ] Bring happiness to the world through writing or poetry?
- [ ] Get everyone to plant at least one tree to save our forests, like Wangami Mathai?
- [ ] Make a million dollars so you can help support your parents in their old age?
- [ ] Teach other women how to be successful financially to enrich their families and communities?
- [ ] Sponsor underprivileged children to learn to read so they can have more success in life?
- [ ] Become a successful entrepreneur and make enough money to help new innovations in the world of autism, Alzheimer's disease, or cancer?
- [ ] Invest in your children's education so they can have a better life than you did?

The fact that you are alive today is not a mistake. You've got a story. You've got a purpose. Wake up every day with a fire in your belly. The ordinary just won't do anymore.

Be Unstoppable!

Mofoluwaso Ilevbare, a.k.a. the *Unstoppable Life* Strategist, is an Energizer, Best-Selling Author, Speaker, and Life Coach dedicated to helping others find their bold identity and be unstoppable at work and life without jeopardizing life balance.

Mofoluwaso is a testament of God's faithfulness. She has been to death's doorway and back, not once, but thrice in her short life! Her commitment to make an indelible mark in the world inspires her to see every day as an awesome opportunity to help others get rid of fear, stress, and anxiety so they can be truly authentic and enjoy great success.

A soulful thought leader, wife, and mother of two, Mofoluwaso is proud to profess she loves God, family, life coaching, and also has a healthy appetite for chocolate cake. She is a member of the John Maxwell Team, a Cherie Blair Women Mentor and has been featured in the Huffington Post, Executive Women, and Channels TV Nigeria. She's co-authored four Amazon best-sellers and also written seven books of her own including the Amazon Best-Sellers *Confidence Pearls* and the *UPLIFT* series.

If you are ready to kick-start your dreams, here are five steps to get you started bit.ly/thisisyourmoment

Facebook: @coachmofoluwasoilevbare

Instagram: @mofoluwaso_ilevbare

Website: www.mofoluwasoilevbare.com

Step Into Your Soul's Purpose
By Justina Ford

There are so many life circumstances that explain why I've chosen to work in the field of coaching, artistry, and healing while doing so as an entrepreneur. I went to college; I got the master's degree. I could do this scope of work from an office, clocking in on someone else's clock. But my "why" revolves around operating in the will of God, honoring and cherishing my values, my family, and serving my divine soul-clients.

I remember when I used to feel so unfulfilled and lost. I thought I had no purpose; I believed that being fulfilled in a career would never happen for me. I had the pressure and weight of holding the title of a first-generation American. My grandmother came from Barbados with an 8th grade education to make a better life for the rest of my family. A strong education to become a lawyer or doctor was the only path that my family could see for me. As early as three years old until around age 16, I had a vision that drew me to the art of the beauty industry. I was good at hair and makeup. I loved how people really opened up and showed you who they really were while going through the process. I loved the freedom, autonomy, and expression of creativity. Yet with even the slightest expression of this desire, I was shut down immediately by my family.

At an early age we have an innate knowing of what our God-given purpose involves. This knowing can be nurtured and developed with love, or it can be shut down like a ton of bricks falling on that dream. For a child, the intuition and ability to make decisions for themselves are questioned, burdening them for years to come. This shutdown is exactly what happened to me. The desire to be a people pleaser stunted any confidence I tried to build, because when my family told me "no," I made the critical choice to follow what was right for them, even though it was wrong for me. This pattern continued far too long in my life. Young people need to feel acceptance when they make choices that they feel are right for them, or they end up becoming spouses and parents who are empty and undecided. That is the trajectory that my life took. But thank God for his gift of healing and transformation.

I went to the college that my parents picked for me. It never even occurred to me that since I was the one who had to pay the loans, I should be choosing the college that I wanted to go to. I found myself deviating from their rules and expectations by studying psychology and human service counseling instead of medicine. This was another variation of my passions, even if not the initial one. I even took it one step further to deviate by finding myself working in topless bars. Making thousands of dollars a week while in college, settling for a degree I didn't really want, was my way of numbing the pain around feeling unheard and powerless. God has truly healed my life in this area.

The rebellious years behind me, one child, and a husband later, I went straight into my field of youth case management, but another dissonance arose in my life. This was another career that didn't quite feel right to me, so I had to make some choices. The tug and pull of giving my children what they needed versus being at work was unsettling for me. I always felt bad about calling into work when my children were sick. And secretly there was this world that I fantasized about where I could work for myself, have a rewarding career that paid amazingly, and be there when my children were learning new things, sick, or simply wanting my attention. In my head, I believed a life like this existed, but in my reality and realm of consciousness, it seemed so far away.

I went on like this for about a year, but when my second child was born, I had to make a hard decision. Did I want to go back to work and only have the first six weeks of his life to spend quality time with him, or did I want to be a stay-at-home mom? Never in a million years did I want to be only a stay-at-home mom, not with the pressure of desiring to be a career woman and make something of myself so my family could be proud. That was never in the cards for me. But when I looked in the eyes of my little baby boy those feelings began to change, and I made that dreaded call to let my manager know I wasn't coming back. Still I knew I was ambitious, I had talents, and I was meant for more than the title of stay-at-home mom. By the time my son turned three months, I was already dabbling in network marketing. I found an amazing company that promoted green living and I did well. I remember my first check and how amazing that felt to get money in the mail while staying home with my children.

The road to walking in your purpose is an ever-evolving one, and right when you think you may have it figured out there is another lesson to be learned. Cherish those lessons and be grateful, because they are propelling you further than you can ever imagine.

I stayed with this company for awhile before that feeling of wanting more starting to sneak up on me. I still felt like there was more to me than getting on the phone and promoting someone else's vision. Yes, I loved healthy, green living promoted by the company, but it was only a part of me. It only filled my desire of making extra money but it did not complete the whole of me. You see, as a multi-passionate woman of faith, I was called to try quite a few things in this life, but at the time I didn't see it as a blessing. I used to feel guilty about wanting more or being on that pursuit for more. If you find yourself sampling life right now, I challenge you to look at it as a blessing. You really do end up finding out who you are and what you are called to do in this life. So sample away and allow God to redirect you where He sees fit.

As I began to deal with this desire for more coupled with the feeling of guilt around wanting more, I became depressed. Who was I to want more when I had a beautiful family, beautiful home, and all my needs were taken care of? Even though the picture looked harmonious on the outside, I was screaming for life on the inside. I specifically remember days when I visualized myself walking down the road. In my mind this was the only way to truly get away. Part of me wanted to get so far away that in my daydream I'd wish someone would just hit me with a car. Those used to be my weekly visions and thoughts. I was so overwhelmed with my decision to stay home with my kids. But I felt guilty for wanting more; I felt guilty for not fully enjoying the stay-at-home role with joy. I should have felt blessed to be able to do this, right?

But we feel things for a reason. Trust those inner feelings, delve into them, check in with them, and journal about them. Spend time with those feelings, acknowledging that God your Creator places them there and allows you to feel them.

I knew I needed to break free from these negative thoughts, from these ideas, from these visions, or they would consume me. I knew too well the feeling of being consumed by the desire to be fulfilled. I knew I wasn't operating from my soul-purpose and it drew me to the point of visualizing about suicide. This innate knowing caused me to self-sabotage to the point of picking fights with my husband out of jealousy. I know the feeling of wanting so much more for yourself, but you don't know how to get there. This is why I do the work that I do today. I will not stand by while another woman feels unworthy, confused, and indecisive about what action to take in order walk her true and divine calling.

I understand that the path isn't straight and narrow. It's a winding road with many pit-stops, but for me to have had encouragement, motivation, a sounding board, and inspiration along the way would have been so healing. If I could have had that winding, sometimes never-ending road be shortened by someone investing time and effort into my calling; that would have been a game changer. It would have saved me 13 years of avoiding the one thing that I knew I was called to do from the age of 16. There is some sort of creative-based soul-purposed work within you as well. And you may need the guidance and support from a community of women, from someone who has been there, from a coach.

My vision took time. It took digging deep in the word of God for myself, actually doing the inner work, and allowing God to prune me and shape me. It took stepping outside of the box and joining the mission of redeeming energy psychology for the kingdom of God. I remember that I had to change my entire mindset around what I was taught to be "wrong." As women of faith we sometime believe that the closer to enjoyment the further from devotion. I had to overcome old beliefs and replace them with new ones. I literally reframed one limiting belief after another and finally decided that I was done. I was done being this Negative Nancy, always finding reasons to tell myself, "No you can't do that," instead of a resounding, "YES! You can go after what you desire!" Make a decision for yourself today! Right now while reading the words on this page.

That decision was a game changer for me. I realized that the God I serve wanted me to live a fulfilled life. The God of the Bible does care about your desires, and He in fact placed them there. He actually has a purpose for each and every single one of us!

I tackled one desire at a time. I transitioned from a woman seeking to please others, into a brave little soul that stepped out on faith to become an aspiring makeup artist with the tagline, "So Much More Than Makeup." I didn't always know what that "So Much More" was. But I fell into the more and allowed the Holy Spirit to reveal to me the passion for emotional healing. Now, I'm an aspiring makeup artist who functions as a Marketing Team Stylist of multiple corporate brands, a Christian Mindset Coach, and Best-Selling Author. Ironically I actually do makeup for a lot of medical TV commercials, applying makeup to doctors and their patients. I was born to be multi-passionate, an entrepreneur, and I've allowed my brand to expand into mindset and energy coaching, utilizing the same Jesus-honoring holistic healing that got me through my own difficult times.

So your path may look a little crazy right now, but that's just because you've stepped off the path perceived...that straight and narrow path that people want you to walk so that they can live their life through you, so that they feel secure that you operate in their definition of success. Step out and find your own definition of success and own it. If I can show up in this epic and empowering manner so can you. God desires that you show up so He gets the glory in your life. He's given you the resources that you need to walk in your calling. It could be a mentor, a coach, a book, a blog, a friend that inspires you. I have utilized a combination of all these resources to aid me in walking in my purpose.

I believe in you, and I know you can do it.

Justina Ford is a Christian Mindset Coach. She teaches entrepreneurial-minded women of faith how to overcome their limiting beliefs, find their confidence, and utilize their God-given talents. Through her work, clients have experienced personal and professional breakthroughs that allow them to overcome limiting beliefs, embrace their self-worth, and monetize their divine passions. She believes real beauty starts with you. Now is the time to embrace the value of your uniqueness so you can propel forward and operate in your purpose.

Justina holds a Bachelor's degree in Psychology, a Master's in Human Service Counseling focused in Business, and additional training in the Emotional Freedom Technique and Splankna Therapy. She also serves as a Marketing Team Stylist, providing her first love, professional hair and makeup services. She has worked with clients such as South Magazine, Coastal Living Magazine, Toyota, Fox 8 News, and Target Stores to name a few. She is a Huffington Post Contributor and Contributing Author of *Notes to Younger Women.*

Join her Free Masterclass: A Heart 4 God & a Mind For Business, The 7 Incredible Mindset Shifts to honoring the ability to having a heart for God and mind for business, at bit.ly/heart4god2

You can join her free community at www.facebook.com/groups/purposefulpursuit

And visit her website at www.justinaford.com or email her at Purposefulpursuit@justinaford.com

My Successful Transition from Academic to Business Owner
By Mike Barnes

How much time do you think a typical PhD candidate spends considering what path they will take after graduating? Having spent 7.5 years in graduate school, I can tell you it is almost none. I don't remember many discussions about what to do afterwards. Almost all discussions that I do recall revolved around getting a post-doctorate position and pursing an academic career. Only a few discussions touched on working for government (this was okay if it was the NIH) or industry (Ack! EVIL!).

What I don't recall hearing, even a single time, was the possibility of becoming an entrepreneur or owning a business for myself. The idea of venturing out and starting a company was not ever discussed.

I want to let you know that, not only is this transition possible, it can be one of the greatest decisions you make in your life. Leaving the comfy confines of academia for the sometimes cold and lonely path of business ownership can be intimidating. But if you press forward, and get a good mentor, you can upgrade life for yourself, your family, and your world!

As I look back along my path, I realize what a disservice it was to me that there was no discussion of business ownership. I was never satisfied doing academic work, with its constant struggle to "publish or perish." Even though I was in one of the top groups in the world in my field, there was always concern about where our money would come from after the current grants ended. What would Congress do with funding? Today, given the chaos rampant in Congress, I can only imagine how difficult conditions must be for academic researchers.

But, I followed the path laid out for me. I got a post-doc position at Cincinnati Children's Hospital and became a research professor. I developed the Cincinnati Biobank and a project called Better Outcomes for Children where we asked for permission to use leftover clinical samples for research. We became a national and international model for how to collect samples. I gave talks around the world and helped others develop similar programs.

Eventually, though, I realized that I really wanted work with a more applied focus. Research is great, but when you don't see results for 10-20 years it can be hard to keep up the energy. So, I made the decision to move to a genetic testing company, Assurex Health. This company was built on technology licensed from Cincinnati Children's Hospital and the Mayo Clinic. We helped people get on the right medication for ADHD, PTSD, or depression as quickly as possible.

I had many people question my path. Most people from academia with whom I spoke reacted with curiosity or even hostility. "What, are you a money grubber, now? Why would you help industry? They're evil! They only succeed because they have tons of money." I received a dozen other comments designed to impugn the character of anyone who went into industry.

After I started working at Assurex, one less hostile question I got repeatedly was "How do you find working in industry?" My answer was, and still is…the biggest difference is mindset. The mindset that academics have is typically one of slow, plodding progress. Progress that often has little direct or immediate impact on the world. For example:

- In academia, it is typical to think and discuss and contemplate and plan *ad naseum*. In business, decisions have to be made quickly, nearly instantly in many cases.
- In academia, rules rarely change. A professor gets her grant and is set for five years. In business, rules and laws can change in a day. Competition can emerge or customer expectations shift in a day. You must be nimble.
- In academia, there is little training, experience, or expectation regarding managing people or budgets. In industry, you are expected to manage well, and there is always an accountant looking over your shoulder.
- In academia, if you publish and get your next grant, that defines success. In industry, the company must make a profit by providing something "the market" is willing to pay for.

I found good and bad people, smart and not smart people, friendly and not friendly people in both academia and business. But I LOVED the new mindset! I have always been someone to "get it done" and I found many others with this mindset in industry.

I eventually realized that the environment of Assurex was still not quite right for me. When I looked around and considered my next step, I thought about becoming a consultant, the only entrepreneurial path I had previously heard discussed. However, I kept my options open and became intrigued when I learned about the field of "Business Coaching".

In brief, business coaching involves helping business owners achieve their dreams. I do that by providing: 1) Awareness of new opportunities the owner might not see; 2) Education they might not have gotten; and C) Accountability to ensure they complete the work needed to move their business forward.

As I look back, I understand how valuable this business knowledge would have been for me and others in academia. Although few will admit it, academic research labs are essentially small businesses. The Principal Investigator (PI) is responsible for budgets, HR, processes and procedures, supply chain, quality of work product, and all the other functions typical business owners handle. Sometimes the PI gets support from the institution, but for the most part they are left on their own.

I know this experience is common across most institutions. While building the Cincinnati Biobank, I felt that I was alone trying to figure out how to build this business. I learned, however, that most in the field felt the same. There were multiple conferences centered on making biobanking economically sustainable, and at essentially all conferences sustainability was a major topic of conversation. I realize now that building biobanks was simply done backwards. Rather than figure out what the market wanted and providing that service, biobanks were built as the institution or investigator wanted and they had to search for users or customers.

Because of my experiences in academia, I have a passion for helping academics flourish in business. Academics have dedicated their lives to learning their craft. They are typically motivated by the desire to improve the world. However, while they are motivated and hardworking, they are not trained in the best practices to make their businesses as successful as possible. That's where I come in.

The strategies that I provide cover the entire spectrum of business from startup to completion: from getting the basics in place, to increasing profits, developing systems and teams, and even transitioning out of the business. All are topics that those in academia need to learn along with many more.

I have learned many lessons that I share with others who are considering building their own business. A few of these are:

- You must be ready to act immediately.
- You will never have full information but must still make decisions.
- There is no safety net. When you own a business, you succeed or fail on your own.
- Networking is a must. In business, you must be able to talk to people and establish relationships.
- You MUST learn to sell your idea/product/service. No one will make others buy from you.
- Selling is based on emotion. You must connect with your prospect on an emotional level to sell.
- Being smart and/or right will NOT guarantee you success. In fact, trying to convince your prospect that you are right (which they will inevitably perceive to mean they are wrong) is almost guaranteed to lose you the sale.
- The market decides. It doesn't matter what you think of your product or service, if the market doesn't want it, you will not make money.

The biggest shift in mindset is to realize that your success and failure are 100% yours. You have FULL ownership. There is no one else to blame. Your competition operates under the same circumstances as you, and some are succeeding. It is up to you to figure out the secret formula for your success and implement it. Getting a mentor hugely increases the speed and likelihood of success.

With all these changes, you will go through an emotional rollercoaster. Even the most prepared entrepreneur has challenges. Those who come out of the cocoon of academia have these challenges multiplied.

By now, you are probably asking yourself a number of questions. Here are just a few I have received:

> With all these negatives, why would anyone want to do this? The truth is that only certain people should pursue business ownership. I chose it because I have a passion for it. I love the challenge. I love the freedom. I love the chance to make an independent impact on the world.

> What are the rewards? Obviously, there are monetary rewards. The freedom and responsibility you get with the mantle of business owner are also rewards. The excitement of building a legacy for your children, and the joy of providing goods and services needed by your friends and neighbor cannot be described. The pain of failure is poignant. The taste of victory is even more sweet!

> What is the likelihood of success? Not good, to be honest. Only about 9% of businesses succeed over 10 years. The good news is that a major factor in success is getting outside advice and support soon enough.

> What does success look like? As a business owner, that is entirely up to you. You might be looking to make lots of money. Or maybe you want to make an impact on the world in a certain way. You define success however you want. You are the boss after all!

> I am motivated by helping others. How does that fit in? This is also entirely up to you. How do you want to help others? Maybe you want to help them build their business through marketing. Maybe you want to

help through accounting, law, plumbing, or anything else. You could choose to build a business to help women find employment or provide a portion of your profit to help people gain skills to reenter the job market. The ability to help others is limited only by your imagination.

There are certainly many negatives to business ownership. At the same time, for the right person, business ownership is an incredible opportunity. Just as when you plan an investment strategy, you must decide for yourself what level of risk you can tolcrate and if you can handle the swings of fate that attend being a business owner.

While I certainly encourage those interested in going into business for themselves to join me on this journey, be forewarned. You have to undergo a monumental shift in knowledge, being, and behavior to be successful. Find a mentor who can help you through this transition. Having gone through this transition myself, I am perfectly suited to guide you. Don't try it alone like I did. Feel free to reach out and let's talk.

And keep in mind…Business ownership is NOT the path to the dark side. It is the path to potential freedom and changing the world as you desire!

Michael Barnes currently lives in Cincinnati, is a father to two wonderful children, as well as an entrepreneur and business success coach. His transition from academia and the Cincinnati Biobank to owning his own business and coaching other business owners to succeed has taught him the importance of developing and keeping the right mindset. His experience building the Cincinnati Biobank and interactions with others around the world as they did the same thing taught him that, although we often feel we are unique with our struggling, most business owners grapple with the same topics. His passion is to help others gain the skills and make the proper mindset changes necessary to transition from employee to business owner with a special emphasis on those coming out of academia.

You can reach Michael at michael@barnesbusinesscoaching.com.

Season of the Soul
By Simran

I was busy making a name for myself in the Entertainment Industry, when I was diagnosed with an arthritic condition called Pseudogout. Pseudogout (PG) is a combination of uric acid and calcium deposits that gather in-between the joints. It creates excruciating bouts of pain, paralyzation, and swelling that last three to seven days. The attacks favored my knees, and most of the time came without warning. The average target age for this incurable, progressive disease is eighty-years old, but I was only thirty-five when I was diagnosed.

PG was not an easily managed chronic illness to deal with while working on several careers in the film industry. My pace as a Production Makeup Artist was slower after three surgeries on my hand. My knees buckled unexpectedly, and I became a fall risk as a Promotional Model. Seven years later, the disease continued to progress, and my attacks happened more frequently. It debilitated my body, making it even more difficult to commit to anything that wasn't in the now.

Shortly after producing a feature film at the end of 2014, I found out that I had two cancerous tumors on my vocal chords, cancer of the thyroid, parathyroid, and lymph nodes. Doctors performed surgery to remove the infected areas and prevent further spreading. This was recommended after six months and is an accepted form of energy medicine used today by Western Medicine. I received my radioactive iodine treatment in June. After treatment, my body was toxic and radioactive, and I was advised to stay away from other people for six weeks. I resided in a five-bedroom home, with family, off conservation land in Framingham, Massachusetts. I decided to pitch a tent outside our backyard and camp there for the six weeks. What I discovered was much more than just somewhere to pass the time.

My support system consisted of family, friends, and Kamala Soul Circles, a woman's group I referred to as my hive. Kate, the head of Kamala Soul Circles was most supportive. She lent me an enormous, white, double-sided, party tent. She and her husband kindly assembled it not too far from dozens of pine and oak trees. I decorated the tent with ambiance and pizzazz, stringing colorful Christmas lights on the top of the outside bars of the tent and draping them around the borders on the inside. Not only did this rainbow-lit tent protect me from the rain, it brought character to the neighborhood. I hung an abundant assortment of scarves and flowing tapestries from the two open sides which provided me complete privacy. From the north of the tent dangled a solid, five-rod, metal wind chime, and at the south of the tent, a dream catcher. There was an art area set up to paint, a table and chairs to eat at, and a foldaway mattress bed which transformed into a couch. Also located inside the gigantic tent was a smaller blue tent, designated as my sleeping quarters. The week was spent filling it with a variety of necessities and heartfelt tokens from my loved ones.

I arrived at my tent after receiving the radiation and fell asleep for almost 24 hours. On awakening, it was a very hot in the blue tent. There was a fan in there, but my body was completely lifeless and I was crawling out of my skin. The synthetic thyroid replacement wasn't working. The doctors prescribed me medication of over 25 pills a day. My conditions caused me severe neuropathy and stiff aching muscles. After radiation, the feelings were even worse. I could barely move. My symptoms were heavy limbs, thinning hair, dark circles under the eyes, depression, and cold sweats. To make matters worse, I began to have a Pseudogout flare-up. All I could do was lie there, breathe, and cry out to God in pain.

A year prior to radiation, I was known as the "go-to" girl for makeup and styling, a local actress on the rise, and I had just produced two movie sets like a BOSS. What a difference a year made. Now totally detached from myself, nothing seemed to interest me. The luster was lost in my life. Worst of all, I couldn't dance or work, and that was everything to me. Becoming angry, I made the decision that I was dying physically, mentally, and spiritually. In the back of my mind thoughts set in that perhaps this was a good time to speed up the process.

Never did I want to suffer while dying, and I certainly didn't want to suffer while living. I worked as a Nursing Assistant for Hospice Care shortly after graduating high school and saw how greatly people with chronic illness suffered. I was sick of taking pills, but this time I wanted to down a handful. I stared at the bottle of oxycodone within my reach. It was next to a bundle of sticks which had a string tied around them, given to me by a woman named Sandy from my hive. My attention gravitated from the pill bottle to the grouped sticks as I remembered what she said when she gave me the bundle. She quoted a great Indian warrior by the name of Tecumseh, (in Shawnee *Tekoomsē* , meaning "Shooting Star.") "A single twig breaks, but the bundle of twigs is strong." Tears flowed down my face. With frustration, I grabbed the group of sticks with my tingling hands and attempted to break them. Sandy and Tecumseh were right; they reminded me of my inner warrior. A warrior chooses bravery, despite the outcome of the battle. Nobody was going to break me but myself. While looking around the tent and noticing the fond keepsakes from my beloveds, I overcame the intense emotional distress of committing the final act. Turning to the heavens, I called upon my higher power and my ancestors to get me through the pain. Exhausted from crying, holding a bunch of sticks to my heart, I surrendered to sleep with the sound of wind chimes dangling above my head.

If only everyone who feels completely alone could realize how supported, involved, and evolved they are. Everything has a characteristic or certain quality that speaks to us. What we encounter communicates to us visually, kinesthetically, or auditorily through vibration or by essence. Gravity is an example of an invisible, mysterious force that supports us naturally by holding us firmly to the ground, yet you won't feel it until you fall.

Besides nuclear medicine, Ancient Chinese medicine is a form of energy medicine that has been practiced for thousands of years and still is used today. The discovery was that the process of healing was conducive to flow and control the Five Elements. The theory of the 5 Elements suggests there's a generating rhythm that follows the law of our essential nature. Fire feeds Earth, Earth feeds Metal/Minerals, Metal feeds Water, Water feeds Wood, and Wood feeds Fire. There's also a control cycle that takes place. Fire controls Metal, Metal controls Wood, Wood controls Earth, and Water controls Fire. This cycle relates to health because in this theory the 5 Elements are associated to specific organs, and these organs are directly connected to emotions. When the elements balance, the organs work at their full function, promoting the best optimum health. Fire rules Small Intestine, Wood rules Liver and Gallbladder, Earth rules Spleen and Stomach, Metal rules Large Intestine and Lung, Water rules Bladder and Kidney. All these rhythms, also known as seasons, have certain qualities and attributes that connect to our inner self and also ourselves to others. The more we recognize our authentic self, the more enlightened our lives become, and we realize that we are all interconnected.

These Elements were there to coach me through everything I encountered. Nature's powerful forces communicated to me by traveling into my thoughts and around my whole being. The season of summer in the tent was the season of my soul. It reminded me that my heart was still beating. The fire within me was proof that isolation didn't exist. Rising like a phoenix created the burning desire to live. Once I realized it, the elements became a synchronized interaction of a divine direction. Like an orchestra and its conductor, they played in synchronicity between the universe and the rhythm of spirit. I was enchanted by the powerful flow cycle of seasonal transition, the art of letting go, letting life flow, and returning to my strength. The awakening had arrived.

 I woke up from a pleasant dream of traveling to an exotic land, and the wind chimes were still. It was almost the break of dawn, and the little rainbow-light reflections faded against the white walls that adhered to the tent's metal bars. Metal is about reflection, letting go, endings, and death. I realized at that moment, parts of me did die that night in the tent, but not all of me. Like a butterfly in her cocoon, a transformation occurred. The earth cradled me, offering her ground to support me. She held me while I recovered and carried my heavy burdens. Earth showed me compassion and assured me that she wouldn't let go of me. Gravity would always bring me back to her.

As the stars started to fade, the big oak and pine trees stood above me. For years they have endured many storms proudly. The forest was cheering me on, with an unending standing ovation. Like the trees, I was the root of our family and epitome of what it was to be boldly strong. I gently let go of the bundle of sticks I fell asleep with and reached for my bottled water. My throat was very dry and as I sipped the water I could feel it going down my throat to the pit of my belly. It refreshed me, and after another sip I fell into deep thought. Perhaps pain is the ending before the beginning instead of the beginning to an ending. Just like the seasons have a process, so does the circle of life. Birth is the ending of pregnancy and the beginning of life. Pain is a signal, the voice of the body. It is present to pull us toward new beginnings and directions.

I unzipped the screen of the tent and slowly pulled myself onto the dewy green grass, and spread out on my back. It was cold, but it awakened me. I deeply inhaled the scents of summer, and exhaled a few AUM's out of my mouth. With eyes wide open, I watched the midnight sky turn light blue, and the sun greeted me. Life seemed much brighter. The squirrels played with each other and the ants marched around their ant holes. I smiled, knowing that solitude isn't a place but an emotion. I wasn't only healing from physical illness; I was there to reinvent myself with divine purpose. I found gratefulness and peace. I found myself in everything and everything in myself.

The Five Elements have become a lost communication for many; slowly unacknowledged, unappreciated, and unrecognized through the evolution of time and the replacement of modern inventions. After my epiphany, it took a couple of days for hope to set in and about a week more for me to start feeling better physically. I enjoyed the Rainbow tent so much that I voluntarily stayed in it for almost four months. My time was spent with studies of self-healing, and I made plans to travel to Indonesia.

While scheduling my itinerary, I came across healthcare pioneer Donna Eden, Founder of Eden Energy Medicine on the internet. I practiced the holistic exercises she taught that helped the body heal and become balanced. Three years later I was cancer-free, traveling the world and about to graduate the Eden Energy Medicine Certification Program. With a heart and hand full of gratitude, I now work with those in crisis as a Soul Mentor, Transformational Coach, and Energy Medicine Practitioner. Energy Eccentric is a movement I created, with my soul name Simran, to assist others in balancing their lives independently through unconventional services and practices. It was ultimately Energy Medicine that pulled me through surviving cancer and living with Pseudogout.

Understanding the Five Elements brought evolution and revolution into my life. As the great Warrior Tecumseh also said, "Live your life so that the fear of death will never enter your heart." Instead of becoming a victim, I learned how to become a warrior, a victor, and ultimately a visionary...a change-maker for all of creation.

Simran had a dream to travel the world while recovering from illness. On her journey, she learned ancient healing techniques. Simran received her spiritual name from Nirinjan Kaur while studying Kundalini yoga. She chose to use Simran as her alias rather than her birth name to honor her own personal awakening. Simran is Sanskrit, derived from the word *smarana*, "the act of remembrance, reminiscence, and recollection." It reflected the highest aspect and purpose in her life.

Her work as a Community Educator, Addiction Specialist, Rape Crisis Counselor, Domestic Violence Advocate, Transformational Coach, Energy Medicine Practitioner, Writer, Minister, and Soul Mentor have created her a place of value and versatility among her peers in the Healing Arts.

Simran has been featured in publications such as RI Health & Wellness Magazine, and more. She utilizes the 5 Elements theory to balance mind, body, and spirit while facilitating change for her clients.

For more information about Simran, her story, and her services, visit www.energyeccentric.com

Discovering My Life's Purpose through Personal Transformation
By Anya Connolly

I landed in Austin, Texas in 1997, from my year-long Professorship at Hallym University in South Korea. I had taught various levels of English Foreign Language classes, as a launch into my career just after completing my Master's degree and turning 30 years old. While I enjoyed this time as an educator in Korea, I recognized that my students, others faculty members, and my engagement in everyday activities in the small Korean town where I lived, all taught me something invaluable as I experienced an entirely different culture and way of life from my own. I was also confronted by an overwhelming sense of isolation and lack of belonging, not only in South Korea, but anywhere. I no longer knew where my home was in the world.

Suffering from another culture shock, the move to Austin seemed just as hard as moving to South Korea, made worse by the challenge of finding a job and having to depend on my boyfriend for a place to live. Once I found a job, I moved into my own apartment, and my boyfriend and I decided to break up. We missed the inner resources to bridge our differences and create a vision for a future together. So there I was alone again, having to learn a new place and find a way to make friends and truly begin to build my life.

My sense of isolation led to my experience of having an existential crisis, so I started reading spiritual books voraciously. I went for long walks daily; reviewing my life, my beliefs, asking myself why was I here, what was my purpose? I felt like I needed a guide to assist me in uncovering what I had yet to discover within that felt so powerful yet unseen and unexpressed. I soon discovered that Neuro Linguistic Programming (NLP) training was offered locally, and I signed up hoping to work with others to develop inner resources to heal and support my well-being, and to reveal my life's purpose.

The spiritual books and training nourished an aspect of me that was starving for more meaning and clarity, offering me glimpses of belonging and purpose. I recalled "mystical" experiences I had felt as a child where I experienced a profound connectedness with everything. Yet this sense of belonging and purpose was not sustained within me, and I longed for more. My study of NLP offered processes that guided me to my internal resources, creating a better understanding of my inner world, my experiences where my beliefs formed, and how they impacted my life.

One of my personal discoveries was that I held a limiting belief that I was alone, and no one was there to support me. I used the NLP techniques to heal this perception and change this old belief to a new one that I am loved, people care about me, and are willing to help me. It wasn't long after this inner shift that I began to feel like I was emerging from the depths of the abyss, that I had a place to call home, and I actually had loving people with whom to share my world.

I saw other changes happening in my world as I continued my use of the NLP techniques, and my life continued to improve. My salary increased steadily and after a year's worth of NLP training, I landed a new job that doubled what I made previously. At this time, I was working in the high-tech industry, which required constant learning of new technologies and methodologies for me to stay proficient in my work. I led global engineering teams, and the stress of the job began to show in my body. I used NLP techniques to help me cope with this stress, but I knew I needed to get more exercise to ease the effects of stress on my body.

I heard that yoga was great for stress relief, and using NLP techniques I found the courage within me to try this practice that seemed so foreign to me. From my very first class, I knew that yoga was my path, and I developed a yoga practice that changed my body and calmed my mind. Yoga helped me recover from chronic back and neck pain, I lost weight, I had more energy, and I had an increasing awareness of mental clarity and a deep inner peace. As I grew to become a Master Practitioner of NLP techniques, others who saw changes happening in my life began asking for NLP sessions with me to address their own blocks and limiting beliefs, in order to create positive change in their lives.

My high-tech career lasted a decade. There I strengthened my technical and communication skills and learned what it took to be successful in the corporate world. I continued my spiritual and energetic studies alongside this career, as I still felt a longing and a calling to satisfy something deeper in me that my success in my corporate career did not. I discovered a passion for Feng Shui and energy work; I became a Reiki Master. I had always been sensitive to energy. I had felt other people's energy and the energy of environments for as long as I could remember.

In 2006, I journeyed to Ireland on a vision quest to discover my life's purpose. Twelve of us journeyed together on a mission to visit Ireland's sacred sites, to be in sacred energies and allow for a deeper experience of self to emerge. My journey led to an inner activation of a higher vision of life that would not allow me to return to what had come before. My soul began to speak through me.

It was there by a campfire that I sang the Irish lullaby that had been sung nightly to me as a child before sleep, back to the land from which it had come. And it was there that we gathered for an Earth healing meditation that transformed the weather before our eyes and left rainbows all around us. In one of our many meditations, I asked for my sacred name. In my mind's eye, I saw a scroll roll open with Aine written on it. I knew that Aine was pronounced as An-ya. Anne is my middle name from birth, so I began using the name Anya, the phonetic spelling of Aine, to hold the significance of my time in Ireland and the profound inner transformation I had experienced.

At the close of 2006, my high-tech job ended, and I knew it was the end of an era. I became a Certified Feng Shui Practitioner, and decided to sell my house so I could travel to India and Thailand, the next leg of my spiritual journey. I used my Feng Shui skills to make my house energetically clean and attractive, and it went under contract in 16 days from being listed on the market.

India was also life changing. I spent most of my time there in an Ashram-type setting, meditating, receiving spiritual teaching and guidance, and receiving a very powerful, blissful, sacred healing energy blessing called Deeksha. The Deeksha energy offered me a blissful experience of oneness, of connectedness to all of life, which felt to me like the true nature of reality beyond my experience of the limitations I held within.

I was taught to how to give Deeksha to others. One day, I traveled to a beautiful temple in the country-side near Chennai, where I began praying and chanting with the others. People looked at me with curiosity and smiled when they saw me chanting with them. The day was very hot so I got a drink and sat under a tree to rest, closing my eyes. When I opened my eyes, three women stood before me, one speaking to me in a language I did not understand and gesturing with her hands. Another woman spoke English and told me, "She wants you to give her the blessing."

The energy ran through me powerfully as I held my hands above this woman's head, and I saw tears running down her cheeks as she received it. I had tears as well. When the energy was complete, I looked up to see an entire line of people waiting to receive the energy. I offered it to each one as they came forward, and the line did not go down. I spent hours that hot afternoon offering this sacred energy.

I've had the incredible fortune of having profoundly rich life experiences such as this that led to my personal transformation and an undeniable awareness of my soul's purpose and authentic expression. I recognize that each experience has been the greatest mirror and teacher for me to remember who I truly am and to powerfully live my purpose. My journey led me to a greater awareness of the tremendous inner landscape of resources and possibilities that I continue to utilize for my continual growth and happiness, and this is what I wish to share with my clients.

My soul's purpose is to assist others to remember who they truly are, to know their authentic power and infinite being by overcoming limiting beliefs and allowing openings and shifts in their mindsets to create a focused, loving, and vibrant life of their dreams. As I've worked with others over the last decade, I've seen amazing results: clients overcoming traumas from the past and powerfully moving forward with clarity on dream projects and life purpose; clients reporting better relationships and improved health; more money and resources becoming available to clients who were seeking more abundance. Nothing brings me greater joy than offering this service to others who are ready for living authentically and powerfully, creating a life of their dreams.

Anya Connolly, M.S. is an Ordained Minister, a Transformational Life Coach and Master Practitioner of NLP, a Feng Shui Master, a certified Holographic Sound Healer, and Reiki Master. She is certified as both a Hatha and Kundalini Yoga Instructor, and is a certified Access Consciousness™ Bars Facilitator.

Anya provides transformational coaching and energy sessions for shifting limiting beliefs, supporting body-mind-spirit awareness and integration. She also works with clients in their homes and businesses to create sacred and energetically supportive living and working spaces.

Sessions with Anya generate a profound authentic inner alignment with one's personal goals and dreams, supporting powerful manifestation of greater Happiness, Health, and Prosperity.

You can find out more about Anya at Thrivealignment.com

It All Starts With a Decision
By Shaneil Stewart

How many of us *want* a better life? We *want* more love; we *want* more joy; we *want* more money, more time, more impact, more influence.

Everybody wants, but wanting is never enough. There comes a time when we must make the decision to change; we must decide we can have the things we truly desire.

I was 15 years old when my mother died. It was January 2006, and I just knew my life would never be the same again. Even though her death was one of the most painful experiences I have ever had, it really was the best thing that ever happened to me.

No, she wasn't a horrible mother; in fact, she was, in my eye, the world's best mother. How could it be then that losing her was the best thing that ever happened to me?

Losing my mother taught me a few things.

It taught me that life was short. She was only 41 years old when she died. It showed me that we have only one life to live and so we have to make it count. But most importantly, her death showed me I could actively make the decision to help change people's lives and leave a legacy; even if I left the world, the lives I touched and the impact I made would long outlive me.

It was Saturday, January 21, 2006, and I stood at the cemetery, watching as they lowered my mother's casket down into the ground. I could sense all the eyes watching my little sister, my dad, and me. I could even sense the arms waiting to hold us in case we started to break down…

…but I was dry.

I didn't shed a single tear that day. The truth is I couldn't. I needed to be strong for my little sister. So, I distracted myself and thought about everything else, except the fact that my mother had just been laid to rest.

For years I blocked out so many memories from that day, yet one thing never left me; I remembered the busloads of people who travelled to her funeral from far and wide to pay their respects.

I knew my mother was a people person; in fact whenever I would go out walking with her as a child, we would stop ever-so-often because people always wanted to talk with her. I look back and laugh now, because a regular ten-minute journey would take us an hour. It used to bother me growing up, but now I think of it with joy as I fondly remember her.

Somehow, I can't help but feel that after my mother passed away she handed me the baton, because even at her funeral so many people came up to me and stopped me just as they would to her before. Of course, they shared condolences, but the other tidbits they shared changed my life forever!

"Shaneil, your mother changed my life," they said. I even remember one man telling me he was going to commit suicide, but my mother was there for him and encouraged him, literally saving his life. I was amazed. I knew all along she was special, but how could one woman truly have such a massive impact on so many lives? Could one woman create ripples across the world of inspiration and impact? And if that woman could, and if that woman's blood flowed through my veins… could I?

Up until that point, I acted like a normal teenager, but it was in that moment that I made the decision to be more, to have more, and to do more with the life I had. In truth, no matter how short life really is, we can do a lot with it if we decide to. Hearing those people speak about my mother and learning about the amazing work she had done in their lives intrigued and inspired me.

How could I touch lives and achieve epic work like that? It was as if losing my mother lit a spark within my heart, the spark that turned me into a catalyst.

You see, I believe that every catalyst has a catalyst. Beyoncé had Michael Jackson, and Oprah had Maya Angelou. And for me, well, I had my mother Marcia Elaine Stewart.

Losing her and learning about the impact she made in people's lives and in a multitude of families made me ask myself, "How can I create impact? And how can I change, not just my community, but the world!?" If every catalyst has a catalyst, and if she was my catalyst, could I then be a catalyst for other world-changers? Could I then strive to inspire others and touch lives too? Could I start a domino reaction and possibly, maybe even change the world?

It was worth a shot.

Growing up, I was always considered an overachiever and a natural-born leader, but I never truly lived up to my full potential. However, after losing my mom, it was like an unquenchable fire stirred within me to finally maximize and use my natural God-given talents.

What would happen if I wasn't playing small anymore and put some effort into the work I did? What if I stopped vegging-out on show after show but used my time (the short time I had on this earth) to bless others?

And that was when my journey started. The spark that lit the light of my inner catalyst became a full-blown forest fire!

I started charities helping children with disabilities. I sat on boards for youth development within government ministries. I started a coalition for young people against drug abuse. I was even awarded scholarships for universities and graduated with first-class honours. I held national positions of student government and leadership, sat at tables with ambassadors from numerous countries, received leadership awards from many governments, including Canada, all before my 21st birthday.

I was the complete embodiment of an overachiever. I travelled to Europe and studied for my multiple master's degrees in Denmark, Portugal, the U.K., Poland, and France. I even worked with over 600 individual clients as a social worker, helping them to alleviate poverty, find jobs, start businesses, and gain education and training. One decision after another just led to more impact with every phase of my life. My journey was like a real-life Cinderella story.

Has it all been perfect? Absolutely not. Every catalyst has a journey, and mine, along with the joys, has had numerous pains too. There have been times when I was homeless, sleeping in lockers in train stations in Switzerland; moments when I lived in Paris and though I was surrounded by all the glitz and glam, I was broke. And even worse, I was broken with nothing to eat but dry bread because I couldn't afford anything else.

Even though today I am a successful entrepreneur, a #1 International best-selling author, coach, and speaker, there were times when I went to conferences and hid in the bathroom because I didn't think I was good enough, or I didn't think I fit in, or I worried that people wouldn't like my accent, or because I was black, or maybe they would think I was too young.

But just like that first life-changing moment when I lost my mother, whenever I met any degree of difficulty in my life, there is one thing and one thing only that made the difference.

It is a decision.

I had to make the decision to change. You have to make the decision to change.

Not all decisions are easy, but I had to decide to no longer struggle. I had to decide I could help people, be a leader, change lives without being broke. I had to decide I could be a catalyst and still be paid for my services. I decided I could live life my way. I decided I could let go of fear and judgment. I decided to no longer be invisible. I decided to "#Ownit" and finally be myself, to be unapologetically me, regardless of what others thought. I decided I could remove toxic people and surround myself with the right people. I decided I could let God lead me.

Within two years my income multiplied by ten. I created a tribe of well over 12,000 people from over 27 countries. I sold out my programs, doubled my rates, hosted international live events, and became a #1 bestselling author. I was even featured on Fox, CBS, and NBC.

Now it's your turn. You are reading this for a reason.

So, what's your decision? What do you have to let go of? What do you want? What's your desire? What's your TRUTH? I want to encourage you to really step up and make the decision today.

Because it all starts with a decision.

Shaneil Stewart is an Online Visibility & Marketing Strategist for catalysts, coaches, and creatives. She helps them stand out online and become the #1 Go-To Experts in their industries so they can have more income, impact, and influence doing work they love while changing lives.

Shaneil is also the founder of The Industry Fame Academy, host of Industry Fame TV, a #1 International Bestselling Author, Coach, Speaker, Entrepreneur, and Philanthropist. Her tribe reaches over 12,000 amazing world changers from over 27 countries across the globe, as she helps them to be visible online and create thriving businesses.

To learn more about Shaneil, visit her website at www.irresistibleinyourindustry.com, a place where rock-star world-changers on the rise can learn the ins and outs of the online marketing world, so they can have a massive reach doing the transformative work they love while being compensated for it.

The Struggles Create Strength
By Adaku Ikotun

Choosing a fearless mindset requires an awareness and courage. It's being willing to look from a new angle and do whatever it takes to go from fear into courage. Let me take you a few steps back.

I was born in Nigeria, but I left with my family to come to the United States when I was fifteen. I am now twenty-eight, and the experiences I had in Nigeria allowed me to become a stronger person and have also granted me great opportunities while living here in the U.S.

In Nigeria, a lot of parents put their kids in boarding school so that they learn to be independent and hopefully grow up knowing what they want in life. Boarding school is also meant to be far away from your family so they don't come to see you constantly. Looking back now, I would also say that this is done with the intent to increase the student's independence since they can't rely on seeing their parents every day.

For a moment, I want you to imagine boarding school as a boot camp setup. Boarding school lasts six years, and when you are done, you graduate and go to college. You start in JSS 1 and go through SS6, which, in American terms, is seventh grade through twelfth grade. Throughout this gruesome boot camp, for six years I had very limited time with family and friends. The only family and friends you developed were the ones you saw every day in the boarding school. Your actual family only came on visitation days, which usually fell on Sundays, but very rarely would that happen.

During visitation days, my family would come with food from home, enough for me to take back to my dorm. There's nothing like good home-cooked meals, especially when dorm food tasted horrible. My parents were always prepared for this visit. I won't forget the things my mom usually packed in her visitation bag, things like mangoes, bananas, pears, corn, rice, beans, soup, chicken, tomato stew, cookies, and toiletries. These were items I needed that would last me until I came home again. It was very heartbreaking whenever my family would visit me because it was just for a few hours. I'm very emotional, so each time they left I stood by the gate, waving goodbye with tears rolling down my cheeks. This boarding school experience made me very independent because I had to provide for myself when my parents weren't there to assist with my needs.

My daily routine at boarding school required waking up early at 5am to start my day. My uniform had to be ironed, shoes polished, and everything had to be on point. There were also daily inspections to make sure hair and nails were trimmed in a ncat manner. Once I was set and ready, I then had to cater to the request of my senior (an upper-class person). I mean EVERYTHING had to be done for her. The water for her bath had to be provided, her uniform was ironed by me, shoes polished, bed made, and trash taken out. The expectations from this senior were extremely high, unlike my peers who had seniors assigned to them that treated them right. Her personality made me very nervous especially, when she walked by me, or if I happened to be in the same room with her.

I couldn't wait to be a senior in order to treat my juniors the right way, like they were my own sisters so I could earn their respect. The senior I had was one that abused her power for her own benefit. I was bullied and scared for my life to the point that I did everything for this senior. This senior was a bully and would look for every reason to treat me as her slave and nothing I did satisfied her. This was the one senior that people were intimidated by and no one wanted to serve her but, unfortunately, I had to serve one of the meanest people in the entire school.

One day the whole school had a scarcity of water, and we had no idea how we were going to bathe. I told my senior that there was no water on the campus, yet she insisted that I couldn't sleep in the dorm if I didn't fetch her water. I cried profusely, but I left the dorm in the middle of the night looking for where I could get water. Other seniors went with their juniors to look for water, yet mine refused to come with me. We walked several miles looking for some until 3am. By this point, I was so tired from trying to get her water that I hid, squatting with a friend so my senior didn't see me. Another friend of mine told me that, in order to really fetch water, I would have to walk five miles away from the school; I carried two buckets, one on my head and one with my hand. It wasn't easy, but I pushed through to make this happen. I felt relieved when I would look ahead and realize we were almost back to school. Unfortunately, as I came with the water, other seniors took scoops of water from my buckets, and by the time I got to my dorm, the bucket of water for my senior was only half full. I was terrified because I knew the water wasn't enough for this senior (she was also rather large in size) and she would want to punish me for not meeting her needs because she had demanded that I bring back two buckets for her to bathe.

When I got to the dorm, our conversation went like this:
Senior: "Whose water is that?"
Me: "Yours. I walked five miles to fetch this water!"
Senior: "This water won't be enough to wash my toes, talk less of my entire body so go out there and fill up that bucket!"

I was so upset at how rude, selfish, and unappreciative she was that I showed an attitude walking out of her room. When she noticed this, she called me back and punished me for several hours for defying her. I had to squat with my arms stretched out in the sun for a long period of time. My senior went to her classes while leaving me squatting with my arms stretched out. I was in this position until evening time. In the boarding school environment, the lower classmates had no say in what the senior commanded to be accomplished, and, to make matters worse, she was the daughter to one of the governors in Nigeria! Talk about an abuse of power! What a terrible feeling as a young thirteen-year-old female to be treated in this matter. I had no way to express my concern or to get any justice for how I was abused. I was rendered powerless.

I also had to clean and iron this senior's clothes. One time I cleaned her clothes but didn't get to iron them because I still had to focus on school and study. On the day of one of my finals she wanted to keep me from getting to class by taking my clothes and soaking them in water! I had to borrow my friend's clothes to just barely make it in time for my exam! Despite all she did, I was required to serve this tyrant until she graduated.

Though very rough, boarding school taught you how to be

organized, clean, and how to plan. Mommy and daddy weren't there to rescue me while I was in boarding school. I had to be organized and time conscious. This experience taught me a lot. Life doesn't always hand out cards that are favorable for you, but the tough experiences make you stronger and also build your character when you choose to not give up. Don't ever allow experiences cause you to throw in the towel because your struggles create strength in the future. Every obstacle creates an opportunity. I had to have a game plan and stay focused on doing school, despite the treatment I went through.

After four years of serving an upper class student, I excited to become a senior and by the opportunity to mentor one of the students who were below me. I wanted to make sure that I never treated anyone the way I had been treated. Sadly, when my semester was about to begin, my father switched the game plan and notified the entire family that we would be moving to the United States. My father took me out of the boarding school, but the good news is that I graduated high school and also college with honors here in the United States.

I am forever grateful to God for His mercy and grace. If you looked back and saw the countless punishments I received, you would be alarmed, but that's not the purpose of this story. I wanted to share something that was so deep in my heart, something that I went through for a while and kept it deep down without letting it out. But I think it's time for people to rise up. I believe that every test creates a testimony. In life, you will have things that will cause you to fall and stumble. It's not about how many of these experiences you'll encounter, but it's about you mustering up strength and deciding to always get back up. Don't let anyone's negativity cause you to feel defeated. YOU determine your future. Don't let anyone else define it for you or cause you to lose hope in your dreams.

I want to inspire you to live your dreams without letting any setbacks keep you from your goal. You are more than a conqueror. I love the scripture in Deuteronomy 28:13 that says, "And the Lord shall make you the head and not the tail…" This means that God's plan for your life is for you to succeed, and He has a desire for you to be a leader, even though your current situation may not show this. Hold on, because, it will end up working for your good. What you speak and set in your heart to accomplish will allow you to keep moving forward and will create a positive change in your mindset. Decide that you won't let people break you, but let the experiences make you! I chose a life of freedom. I chose to finish my education and pursue becoming a strong-willed entrepreneur by working on my business. I chose to live out the dream that my Heavenly Father has prepared for me. He's always been there through the good and the bad.

My boarding school experience created inside of me a desire to never give up. I am not going to sit around and allow someone who is ignorant of their own purpose in this world determine my future. I chose to push through all the pressure I encountered. I strongly believe the choices you make determine your destiny and, in order to make a positive impact, I'm turning my story around to be positive instead of negative. I guard my heart because of all the things I've been through, and I live to inspire my daughter so she doesn't experience what I did.

Sometimes God allows you to go through a test so that it becomes a testimony to somebody else. Hopefully my story today will be an eye opener for all those who have gone through physical, emotional, or cyber-bullying in life. Be a voice and not an echo. Rise up and begin to speak, because there's power in your testimony. That's how God gets His victory. Always remember that the struggles you encounter create strength when you never give up. Stay inspired, stay motivated, and choose to always move forward!

Adaku Ikotun is an inspirational and motivational speaker, blog writer, and YouTube personality.

Adaku loves to live life on purpose! Her dream is to share the journey that she's experienced (from her childhood in Nigeria to life in America) to help change the world, one person at a time. She's a wife and a mother who believes that, by sharing what you've experienced in your journey, you are one step closer to helping someone avoid making the same mistakes you've made in life. Her desire is that her story will make a difference in somebody's life.

Youtube: Adaku Inspires
Instagram: www.instagram.com/adakuinspires
Website: www.adakuinspires.com

Coming Back to Creativity
By Karin Anne Davis

Once upon a time I created with reckless abandon and pure joy: puppet shows, forts, spy games on the swing set, and wardrobes for my teddy bear named Wuggy. I didn't have any concept of creativity – it was just fun! Some projects, like the Teddy Bear Olympics, were enormously successful. Others, like the time my best friend Lisa and I built a golf course inside her house by sticking Pick-Up Stick flags into her mother's white shag carpet with Plasticine – not so much!

I loved school – creating stories, playing make-believe, and making art out of nothing. The more obscure, the better. I painted pictures, created imaginary cities, and revelled in being unique.

But it didn't last long.

I soon realized that I couldn't draw very well, so I stopped. I learned that being different wasn't cool or popular, so I conformed. And I started to see that there was a system in school that led to success. So, I followed the rules, stopped asking questions, squelched my curiosity and imagination, and got great grades.

At the same time, I started to lose a part of myself.

By the time middle school came around, I was miserable, sad, and depressed. My confidence and energy vanished. My resilient personality was replaced by one of fear. I continued to follow the ever-increasing rules and procedures at school and was rewarded with high grades. In high school, the trend continued. Even in a specially enriched creative-design program, I found my ability and need to think differently diminishing. I graduated with honours, awards, and early entrance to the University of my choice. But inside I was confused and lost, unable to figure out what I liked and disliked, unable to think for myself. Following the advice of others, I enrolled in a scientific program, reasoning that it would help me land a high-paying job and stability.

Not surprisingly, within a few months of starting university, I crashed. Eventually diagnosed with an eating disorder, depression, and anxiety, I fought with myself to stay alive. Little did I know at the time, this would be the beginning of my long road back to creativity.

During my recovery, I worked hard with my counsellor to figure out who I was, what I was good at, and what gave me joy. I started to think for myself again, questioning what I had learned and believed, and imagining the possibilities ahead of me. I even started to create again, making toys for my young nieces and nephew.

I realized that I had the ability to decorate small spaces with style and ease, coming up with cool ideas to make the best use of space. As I started working doing administration in the non-profit sector, I found that I could see ways of improving systems, making them more efficient and effective. And I surprised myself when I started to look at big challenges, like the high rate of eating disorders among girls, and think of unique ways that I could contribute to the solution.

I started a 'zine before they were even popular back in the 90's, promoting healthy body image and self-esteem to girls and women. I created a presentation and began speaking at schools, educating teachers about eating disorders and how to support their students. I had people frequently comment to me that I was "creative." Yet my immediate reaction was, "No I'm not!"

In my mind, the special label and honour of being creative was reserved for artists, actors, dancers, or musicians. Certainly, not me, who could only come up with ideas like having the organization where I worked (National Eating Disorder Information Centre), partner with the Girl Guides of Canada to create a new badge on healthy body image.

I wish I could say that my recovery was swift and easy. But it wasn't. For every step forward, I would fall back two. I struggled to find myself, my confidence, my passion. My career moved forward at a snail's pace and stalled frequently as I continually found myself needing to prove my skills and abilities without the proof of a university degree. I moved from one counsellor to another and one treatment program to another, making progress in baby steps. I had weeks, months, and years that were better than others. It was frustrating and exhausting.

What I didn't yet understand was the degree of grit and resiliency buried deep inside of me.

For years, I continued to search for my calling in life. I knew that I wanted more than a job, or even a career, and I knew I wanted to help people but I had no idea how! I thought I wanted to work towards the elimination of eating disorders, but I found the work to be too close to home for me. I briefly considered interior design, but realized I'd have to follow the wishes of the clients rather than just design for my pleasure! I considered writing books for children so that I could teach them important lessons hidden in fun and crazy stories.

I fell into the area of health promotion for a while, learning about how social issues like poverty and inequality are determinants of one's health. I learned to use new technology as computers invaded the workplace, and soon thereafter, the mysterious thing called the internet. I enjoyed helping non-profit organizations use this new technology to communicate with their clients and tell the story of their work.

I took these new skills and started working with volunteers, and then in higher education. When I was in a place where I could develop new ideas, I was engaged. When I got stuck in an environment where change was less welcome, I struggled. I often considered the idea of becoming an entrepreneur. The idea of being in control of my own destiny and able to try new things and different ways of working was appealing. The problem, however, was I didn't know what I wanted to sell!

At some point, I came across a program in adult education and was particularly curious about the how technology impacted the field. After completing a Masters Certificate program, I continued to become a Certified Training & Development Practitioner. I loved teaching my peers how to use cool new technology and online programs, and started to focus in on ones that enabled people to be more creative with marketing their programs and services.

I became interested in a growing trend, the intersection of the corporate and non-profit sectors; business for good. Social entrepreneurship and corporate social responsibility were new business models that I found intriguing, and they seemed to be an interesting mix of my skills and my passions. Though, even after immersing myself in continuing education in the field, the lack of formal education and credentials continued to be my Achilles heel. I felt like I was close – but still not quite there.

Around the same time, I started to notice that "innovation" was becoming the buzz word in the corporate world, particularly in technology start-ups. It wasn't long before the word crept into higher education, the public sector, and eventually the non-profit sector. I sought out books, experts, and research on the topic and absorbed as much as I could. I was curious and had a million questions. I craved more. I remember spending all night searching the internet for a course I could take, a program that I could enroll in – something where I could learn more about innovation. I came across a strange site called MindCamp. I signed up immediately, and eight months later I was in Orillia, Ontario at my first creativity conference.

I wasn't sure what to expect, but I made a promise to myself to be open and go with the flow. From the opening session to the closing ceremonies, I was the first person in the room with my notebook and coloured pens. I sat as close to each presenter as I could; I hung on every word they spoke and participated fully in every crazy activity they planned. I was mesmerized.

And I was hooked!

It took some time to process what I had learned – creativity is a field of study? There are theories and models and research? Creativity can be taught and learned? It is possible to be creative and not be able to draw? Creativity is the first stage of innovation? I am creative?

It took more time to figure out how I could use this new information and create meaningful work for myself. I mulled things over, cruised the internet, and read some more books. I asked more questions and imagined what could possibly be.

And then it happened. My calling – my why – my purpose, it all came together. I would teach people that they too could be creative and innovative, even if they couldn't draw. And I would show them how creativity could be harnessed and cultivated in people and organizations, and motivate them to make real change in the world.

It wasn't pretty and it wasn't easy. But I finally found my way back to creativity.

Karin Anne Davis, CTDP, is passionate about creativity, innovation, and making a difference in this world. She believes by embracing and harnessing creativity, each of us can learn to innovate and provide value, whether to a few individuals, a whole community, or the entire planet.

Karin works with people who are passionate about becoming more creative. She teaches them how to build their creative confidence by thinking and acting differently. She helps leaders make the case for creativity at work, and develop a mindset and culture of innovation in their organizations. She fosters and facilitates creativity and innovation in her local community and online around the world.

Her vision is a world where individuals believe in their ability to be creative and innovative, where businesses and organizations embrace creativity and innovation, and where people from all facets of life come together to make this world a better place.

If you would like to find out more about Karin please visit the following link: www.creativityandinnovationacademy.com

Great Things Begin With Gratitude
By Brenda Benalcazar

I slowly walked over to the car not fully knowing what would happen if I turned my back on him. I smiled reassuringly at the nervous faces of my children strapped into their car seats. I put my seat belt on, took a deep breath, and put the car in reverse. As I pulled out onto the street and put the car in drive, I watched him slowly fade out of sight in the rear view mirror.

Making the decision to get divorced wasn't easy, but it was necessary. There were no tears nor regret, only relief and a slight glimmer of hope. I reluctantly drove home to Montana where I grew up. I never wanted to go home again, but I had nowhere else to go. I drove for three days from Chicago with two kids in tow, until I finally reached the place that I had left 18 years earlier to find adventure. I looked at this as a time to re-evaluate and reflect on the whirlwind that had become my life. My children and I moved in with my eighty-eight year old grandmother. I was very grateful to have a safe place for us to live.

As I looked back over my marriage, I realized I had lost myself so much that I didn't feel like a whole person. The person that I was had slowly eroded away, one decision at a time, over a period of years. I lost my voice and fell silent. I decided that year in Montana to feel grateful for the things that I was left with. I was so grateful to be a mother of two children and to be healthy and alive to take care of them. I was also grateful for the new religion that I brought back home that I didn't have when I left. I made a choice to pray and be led by the Spirit, as it had been a constant guide during the previous three years of my life. And I began to trust myself again.

Being home for a year gave me the chance to heal and grow. But then, it was time to move on. The Spirit prompted me to move to Utah. Once the choice was made, everything fell into place, which solidified my conviction to follow the Spirit. I knew that somehow the Lord would provide a way for us to be all right as a family. I didn't know how it would work out since all I really had were my kids, my car, and some clothes. I didn't even have beds or dressers, just a few pillows and blankets. But the Lord works miracles through other people. What I didn't know at the time was that many people heard of my story through friends and decided to help. The day that we moved in was a huge surprise. We not only had an apartment full of furniture and all the supplies necessary to run a household, but clothing for me and my children. I was so incredibly humbled and thankful for all that I was given. Gratitude was a wonderful teacher.

I began to reflect on my children. My son was three years old when my daughter was born. Not long after she was born, I got this overwhelming feeling that something was wrong. Never in my wildest dreams would I have imagined my eight-month old baby girl was dying. Several months later, I heard the four words no parent ever wants to hear, "Your child has cancer." Looking at my sweet baby, I couldn't believe that cancer was in her body and would, according to the doctors, spread and kill her. She was diagnosed with bilateral retinoblastoma, a cancer in both eyes that is also genetic. We were sent the children's hospital in Chicago. Because of the genetic factor, my three year old son had to be tested. I remember feeling the crushing range of emotions from deep sadness and total disbelief as my little children, that I worked so hard to bring into this world, might leave before they even got started. Thankfully, my son did not have cancer. The team came in and met with us, saying that they wanted to remove my daughter's left eye. As the meek person that I had become and having not made a decision in years, I spoke up and said no.

After two years of treatment, my daughter's cancer was once again very deadly. It was growing and about to spread. At this time, a feeling of peace entered my heart to let me know that it was now essential to remove her left eye. I held my sweet baby girl in my arms and walked her down the hallway and gazed deeply into her big brown eye for the last time, sweetly kissed her on the check and handed her over to the nurse. After the doors closed, I broke down and sobbed. She woke up the next day like the child she was always meant to be, free of pain and discomfort. A few weeks later when I took off the bandage and she realized for the first time that she couldn't see, she grabbed me tightly around the neck and quietly wept. Then she pulled away and looked at me, smiled and ran into the next room to start playing. She was two years old.

It was around this time that I started to notice some unusual behaviors in my son. I thought that his behavior was just his personality. I also knew he was having a hard time sharing me with his sister when she had cancer. It was hard for me to wake him up before the sun rose and come home after the sun had set, picking him up from a different house every time I had to be at the hospital with my daughter. It nearly broke my heart when he asked me when it was going to be his turn to go to the hospital. He wanted cancer if that meant that he could spend that much time with me. It also broke my heart when so many people with good intentions said to me that my daughter was such a special spirit in front of my son. The deep sadness in his big brown eyes and the look on his face will be forever etched in my mind.

After my daughter was cleared from cancer and we moved to Utah, I took my son to several types of doctors. He had various diagnoses, but in my gut I knew there was more. Then I finally heard the words, "Your son has autism." I remember mourning for him and being so deeply saddened. It was reminiscent of going through cancer with my daughter. I cried for three months before pulling it together and being grateful that I knew the diagnosis so I could help him. I studied everything I could about autism and even went back to school to study nutrition.

Shortly after my son's diagnosis, I was introduced to and started on a journey of personal development. I began to work through my issues while uncovering some new ones as well. The first lesson I learned was that in order make things better, you get to take full responsibility for your life. This meant that I could no longer consider myself a victim. This concept was life-changing because it meant that I had the power to heal from the past and choose a new course for the future. The second lesson was so much harder. I got to forgive everyone and clear up any ill feelings that I harbored and release them. I also stopped using words like "have" and "need" and replaced them with "get" and "want" to focus more on positivity, abundance, and choice. I started by forgiving myself for all the mistakes I made, and then radiated outward from there until I had no one left that I felt needed forgiveness on any level.

After a year of reading self-development books, I discovered a limiting belief that was created when I was ten years old. We rarely went to church when I was growing up, but I remember hearing the story of Jesus and the rich man. The rich man inquired of the Lord what he could do to inherit the kingdom of Heaven. He was told to sell all his belongings and give it to the poor, then follow Him. The man loved his riches more than he loved the Lord and walked away. I remember thinking that I should just be poor so I wouldn't have to make that choice.

This limiting belief was buried in my subconscious for years and could very easily explain my relationship with money. This tenet was also coupled with the scarcity mentality of my family and generations of having just enough. The ancestral memory written in my DNA housed the memories, anxieties, and fears of my grandmother growing up in the Great Depression. Her fifth birthday coincided with the worst financial crisis of the twentieth century, the Stock Market Crash of 1929. My mother and father both grew up poor, so scarcity and lack held a place in my DNA.

Shortly after this realization, I began to study the law of attraction. Now that I was aware of this belief concerning wealth, I could change it. Advances in science now tell us the theory that our DNA and genes are set in stone, is no longer true. Scientists have also studied the neuroplasticity of the brain and the role between the conscious and the subconscious. Simply put, you can rewire your brain by focusing on what you want. I began to focus on wealth and called into my life my role as a wealth coach. There is no better way to learn something, than to be a teacher. I get to focus all day on helping people accumulate wealth, thus redefining my relationship with money. The most important lesson I learned from practicing the Law of Attraction is that you attract what you are and not what you want. In order to attract what you want, you get to work on becoming the best version of yourself. Through this practice, along with prayer and meditation, I am attracting people that could benefit from what I do; I feel that I am the how many people don't know exists. I am mission-driven to attract those that are searching for answers that I can provide. I love what I do.

Another result of changing my belief was finally getting the books that were stuck in my head onto paper. My children have grown up around pediatric cancer patients and now both are going to be attending a school just for children with autism. They are aware, kind, and accepting of special children, and I want to share our stories with the world so all can become aware and enlightened to the challenges that come hand-in-hand with both cancer and autism. It has always been a dream of mine to be a writer and by doing so now, another wish is fulfilled.

It's incredible where your mind can travel to when you are looking over the roadmap of your life. I am still standing, and have a strong faith in God. I realize that my children are fully developed spirits and have their own unique challenges and gifts. I am their guide and they are my teachers. I am still a work in progress. And I have noticed that great things begin to happen when you are grateful for what you have been given.

Brenda Benalcazar is an entrepreneur, writer, artist, and an advocate for children with Autism and Pediatric Cancer. She graduated with a degree in Fine Art and Theatre from Northeastern Illinois University in Chicago Illinois. She is a certified Integrative Nutrition Health Coach who studied at the Institute for Integrative Nutrition in New York City. She is also a Licensed Wealth Coach with Elite Hathaway. She is very passionate about educating people about money, as well as teaching strategies and concepts to grow, protect, and accumulate wealth.

Brenda is also passionate about writing children's books to bring awareness to autism and pediatric cancer, specifically retinoblastoma. Her first children's book, *Because I'm Awesome*, about her son with autism, is currently being illustrated. She has written a series of books about her son's autism and her daughter's cancer and is looking forward to those being published as well. She plans to donate a portion of the proceeds from her children's books to various charities including Generation Rescue and the National Children's Cancer Society. She is a member of the Church of Jesus Christ of Latter Day Saints and lives in Salt Lake City, Utah with her two children Joshua and Sarah.

You can reach Brenda by email at brendabenalcazar@gmail.com or Linkedin at Brenda Benalcazar,
Follow her on Instagram at brendajoshsarah , or snapchat at brendab2525.

Passion of the Heart
By Janis Melillo

In the darkness of the night, when the house is still and the sultry almost-blue light from the moon shines through the window, I am reminded of its magnetic beauty and that every day is a true blessing. I know that the sun will rise and I am grateful for yet another wonderful day on this amazing earth. I rise before the early bird even thinks about getting the worm and that's okay. It's quite early and yes, it will certainly be a long day, but so worth it!

I stumble out of the darkness into the living room, find my way to my favorite chair, say my prayers, and begin my day with prayers and gratitude. I practice my cleansing breaths and begin to think about what I am going to write in my daily journal. I pause for a moment or two and as I stare at my journal and listen to what is in my heart; the sound of the clock is ticking, the furnace is roaring, the birds to start to chirp away, and I smile. That is the time when the realization of my journal theme for the day comes to me.

It may not be a theme, but just one word that in that moment that describes what my heart is feeling and what my soul beckons me to do. Sometimes I am not sure what this means. It's as though the Universe sends me a message reminding me that my purpose in life is more aligned with what is in my soul. A soul-food kind of purpose. Why at this stage in my life, is the Universe beckoning me to be more, do more, say more? I am not absolutely certain why; I just know that I am destined for whatever the Universe directs me to do. I AM doing just that. Following the rhythm in my heart to help people who desperately need someone in their corner.

In the words of Dr. Wayne Dyer, the phrase I AM, means more to me than I can adequately describe.

I AM a survivor of an assault which is very difficult for me each day. More importantly, I have come to realize I AM so much more than the assault and not defined by that horrific event. Ultimately through the pain, sorrow, and emotions I never knew I had, I have endured only to become stronger and healthier each day. This led me on a path of self discovery and knowledge to learn, do, and be more. I AM a survivor.

It was in a moment of self-despair, about 22 years after the incident that my epiphany occurred. At different times during my life, the events surrounding the evening I was attacked popped up in my memory. I just kept burying them and never wanted to deal with the emotional turmoil I felt. I found solace and comfort in food. A lot of food, more food than my frame could handle. I was the super-size queen and I had the dress size to prove it! It was in that moment when I tipped the scales at over 242 pounds, and I looked at my chubby little face in the mirror that I had my wake-up call – BAM! It hit me in that very moment that I had to take care of myself, physically, mentally, emotionally, and so much more.

The next day, I joined a gym, signed up with Jenny Craig, and bought a dress I wanted to fit in. I transformed my body and my mind and as a result became healthier physically and emotionally than I ever had been! For the first time in a very long time, I took the reins away from fear! I eventually fit in that dress I bought and still have it to this day!

My journey was not an easy one but led me on a path of wellness that I never expected. I was amazed at how I was able to get my health back. I felt better than I ever had - I could walk down the street and not feel exhausted and out of breath. I could be more active without forcing myself. I wanted to be more active and take a walk or hike across the State of Connecticut. Going to the gym each day, I felt stronger and more invincible. I no longer craved all of the junk food I was consuming, but rather craved going to the gym and learning a new exercise or trying the latest gym equipment.

I was hooked! I found a healthy addiction worth its weight in gold! I found that the will and nature of the mind to take the body where it can and should go is utterly amazing! I realized that at any stage in life, the will to change a certain behavior or pattern is obtainable. It's hard, frustrating, and sometimes, or maybe most of the time, you may want to quit, but it truly is something worth working toward.

I was successful in my quest to become healthy and I am very grateful I had the opportunity to change the outcome and future of my health. As such, I became obsessed with fitness and went to school to become a certified personal trainer. I became a licensed massage therapist, a great addition to my résumé. I loved being a personal trainer and massage therapist! Both of these professions complemented each other very well. When I was no longer able to practice those professions due to physical restrictions, I felt very lost. There had to be a way for me to still practice in the wellness industry in some capacity by assisting others. It took me quite a while to figure it out but my next venture proved to be a natural progression.

I became a health coach! I completed my training through the Institute for Integrative Nutrition. I studied and learned about different diet theories and how and why bio-individuality is so important. In short, one person's diet may be another person's poison. Health coaching is not about putting my client on a diet - health coaching encompasses many facets including dealing with the whole person's whole environment: physical, emotional, social, financial, and occupational well-being. All of these factors, though sometimes limiting, contribute to a person's overall wellness.

What does wellness mean to me? I could write a novel! But in the simplest terms possible, wellness is not a one-size-fits-all solution. Wellness engages the mind, body, and soul to work harmoniously together to achieve what you may think is impossible. How do I know this and how can I be so sure? I am living proof that it is possible.

This does not mean that I am perfect. It means that I found the formula that is best suited for my wellness. Losing weight to become healthy is a good thing, but ignoring the underlying issues and problems that got you there in the first place is a form of self-sabotage. I did not realize that I was torturing myself and blaming myself for the trauma I experienced. It was just easier for me at the time to quit and go to the bag of chips rather than face and deal with the trauma I went through.

My passion for wellness led me to begin my on-line health coaching practice. I am able to assist my clients on their path of wellness through fitness and nutrition! To me, there is a deeper connection and satisfaction in knowing that in some small and larger ways I can make a difference in someone's life; to help and assist them on their path of wellness! I consider myself an Ambassador of Wellness!

It's not about the job title though. It's about my client's ability to achieve wellness on their terms. The ability for my clients to obtain what they thought was not possible and the look on their faces when they have - priceless!

I AM not what I thought I wanted to be, but more than I ever thought was possible. I AM a survivor - I no longer have to face that fear; it is gone now, not forgotten but gone in the sense that I don't feel like I have to carry that burden and I no longer feel ashamed nor afraid. Out of the darkness came the light and I work on that light each day!

It is through that light that I am truly blessed to be in a position to assist others; to serve as someone's health coach, their Ambassador of Wellness - that is what is in my heart and soul! To spread the knowledge and plant the seeds for someone who wants their healthy back - that is an honor and privilege I hold dear to my heart!

When you really stop and think about it, I found my passion of the heart and I'm not letting go anytime soon!

Janis Melillo lives in North Haven, Connecticut with her husband, Gary. She is a Transformation/Wellness Coach who works with women on their transformation path towards wellness through fitness and nutrition by implementing small changes leading to a healthier lifestyle overall. She is a certified health coach, having received her training through the Institute for Integrative Nutrition. She is a former licensed massage therapist and certified personal trainer.

Janis hosts a daily blog (Monday - Friday) on Facebook called FitnessDiva-411 where she shares her love of fitness and nutrition. She is also the host of three other Facebook groups: Circle of Hope, FitnessByDesign-411, and GlutenFreeByDesign-411, and is the owner of her health coaching business WellnessByDesign. Her Facebook business account is: @WellnessByDesign411.

Janis is also an ordained minister and recently started Digital Life Ministries, an on-line ministry which may also be found on Facebook. This is a non-denominational ministry that shares quotes and spiritual inspiration.

Along with fitness and nutrition, Janis loves to write, and two books she co-authored hit the International Best Seller List! Her third book was recently published, and she has also written articles for two different on-line publications.

You may contact Janis through her
website at: www.WellnessByDesign.liveeditaurora.com
email: Janis@janismelillo.com
You may also follow her on Twitter: @MelilloJanis.

Playing Against the Hand of God
By Tiki Tikifaces Tunstall

Life is not typically about the circumstances you encounter, it's more about how to play the cards you've been dealt.

The year 1992, was the worst of my life. Sometime around three o'clock in the morning, my uncle and I had to sneak up an employee elevator to the ninth floor of Barnes Hospital to see my mom who was dying of cancer. Before she expired, I walked down the dark, gloomy hallway. My heart was extremely heavy. Before entering Room C, I became hesitant. Inside the room to the right of me, half of my world was dying in a sick bed. Eyes watered down, using one hand as a wiper for my eyes, my vision in life became blurred, taking me to another space in my mind.

As I stood in my mind, thoughts shuffled and dealt out a deck of cards I didn't sign up to play. Hurt, disappointed and confused, I was mad at God and wanted to have nothing to do with Him.

I began to have a vision of me sitting in a BLACK ROOM, dressed in red, a color that represented the permissive will of God. However, God was also in the room dressed in red, being in His perfect will. There was a table, two chairs, and a deck of cards. As I approached the table, the deck of cards shuffled themselves representing my mind and His.

I jumped back feeling a cool breeze out of nowhere. "Everything is all right, come and play," a voice said.

In fear, I decided to follow the voice's instructions. I looked as the cards were dealt. Seven permissive cards were dealt to me and seven perfect cards were set on the opposite side of the table ready to be played.

Sloth, Lust, Greed, Gluttony, Pride, Envy, and Wrath were the cards dealt to me. Labor, Contentment, Generosity, Fasting, Humility, Satisfaction, and Love were the cards on the opposite side of the table.

I finally took a seat at the table. I picked my cards up. On the backside of each card was an inscription that read, THE GAME OF LIFE. God kept His cards on the table.

I looked at my cards and thought how unfair of a hand I had been dealt. No verbal sound came from my end, but my emotions spoke for me.

I was holding the four suits I had worn throughout life. Two spades of sloth and gluttony. A heart of pride. Envy and wrath of diamonds and two clubs of greed and lust, ready to play against the hand of God.

As I held my suits in my hand, God held His in His heart. This is a first; two players are holding winning hands but from two different worlds. I decided to hold my best hand and throw out my lowest card, Gluttony.

After the death of my mom, I lost interest in a lot of things including my appearance. I dressed nicely but really was not into being physically fit, because I drowned my pain in food. Over time, I went from 135 to 215 pounds. It was really depressing and hard to get back on track in life, which led me to another vice: GREED. Due to my greed, I worked from 6 a.m. to 4 p.m. on my main job then worked an overnight job three times a week, which led me to see things coming from the streets while traveling home. Due to living above my means, I worked so hard trying to earn money to keep up with my expenses, that I eventually lost both jobs. Losing those opportunities brought on a new vice: SLOTH. I didn't necessarily become lazy as sloth might imply, but I did lose my zeal in pursuing a career. I was hurt and disappointed. I felt defeated. Now LUST attempted to introduce itself to me. Lust is a quick and easy way that many people rise to the top. However, my issue with lust didn't come from having lots of partners; my issue came from allowing things to get in the way of God. Consequently, I began to focus on gaining material possessions, and PRIDE entered my life. I was so hurt that I accepted pride over God. Though I created and wrote awesome work, God didn't allow my creations to prosper. ENVY entered my life as I became spiteful of others, not because they were inherently better, but because their material was working and mine was not. I published a novella that got great feedback, but due to lack of publicity I was not given the exposure I felt I deserved. I became so angry I began to self-destruct and welcomed WRATH into my personal life. I yelled and became mean because I thought I had the right. I became so mad, God had to intervene.

Revisiting my vision, God changed the game and played His hand. "Let's play this over," God said.

I threw out the orange card, Gluttony. This card had an overweight young lady dressed in orange, with a meal in her hand and food stuffed in her mouth while sitting on a food scale. I turned the card over and it read, "He who keeps the law is a discerning son, but he who is a companion of gluttony humiliates his father."(Proverbs 28:7.) Purposely, I wanted to humiliate God because I felt He humiliated me by taking my mom away.

God then pulled out the light orange card: Self-Control. This card had a young vibrant lady on it, praying with her palms close to her heart while chaos hovered around. God flipped over the card and it read: "I can do all things through Christ who gives me strength." (Phil 4:13.)

Getting antsy and impatient, I threw out the dark green card; the card is Greed. On this card, I saw myself bent over a chair, tired and sleepy, counting money yet losing my life. The back of that card read, "For everything in the world - the lust of the flesh, the lust of the eyes, and the pride of life - comes not from the Father but from the world." (1 John 2:16.) I threw out this card to warn God of the cards I was about to release.

God looked at me with love in His eyes, and threw out a card with a man sitting in a rocking chair holding his tired arms out, and the back of the card read, "So, Jacob served seven years to get Rachel, but they seemed like only a few days to him because of his love for her." (Genesis 29:20.)

I pulled out Gluttony and He Self-Control. I played Greed, He played Patience. I threw down Sloth and He came with Diligence. I challenged him with Lust and He countered with Self- Denial. I diverted myself to Pride and Humility bowed itself on the card game. We continued to throw out cards until we got down to the last two that would determine the winner. I was left holding Envy and Wrath. God held Kindness and Love. I put my cards on the table face-down to rub my legs. I looked at God while He looked at me. He waited for me to play my hand but I waited for Him to forfeit.

I held Envy and Wrath, and God Kindness and Love. I threw out Envy, a green card, that doesn't want to be like God and doesn't want God to be Himself. I stood up and God sat down.

In my envy, I rose from my seat at the table in attempt to exalt myself above God. We stood as equals in my mind, though in my continually failed effort, my anger grew into Wrath and I began to lash out at God. Nevertheless, God remained in His place and though I excreted anger, God radiated love. The more my attacks increased towards Him, the more God's love shone on me until it brought me to my knees. God's enduring faithfulness humbled me past my wrath and caused me to accept His everlasting love. In my life, I accused God and wanted to hold Him accountable for my trials and tribulations. Yet God's love endures forever, and He forgave my every sin and insult. Through His grace I am a changed woman, forever.

I believe God used my life as a prophetic one to show what we do daily and the results we get, when we operate outside of His plans for our lives. I plan to use my experience to minister to those that are not fulfilling their purpose in life. I learned that when we allow God to control our lives and follow His instructions, the lives we created, that seem to be a chaotic journey, will instead be smoother. But we must only submit to the rules of His game that bring victory to all the kings, queens, jacks, and jokers that are assigned to overthrow the hand that is difficult to defeat.

Deaundra Tiki Tunstall is a childcare professional who serves on the Executive Board for childcare with SEIU to bring about a promising future for growing individuals. She is the owner and creator of Tikifaces adventures enterprise that gives kids the opportunity to create their own world through imagination. She is the author of two published books, *Will You Be My Friend?* and, *In The Name Of God, They Serve The Devil.* God blesses her to see into dimensions and gifts her to write stories of it. Being a minister in the church as well in her craft, she is honored to hold dear the voice of God for His people and make sure they understand what has been heard or seen. Deaundra Tiki Tunstall is the mother of Tatyana and two grand girls.

You can reach her at: tikifaces1974@gmail.com or
www.tikifaces.net

Beyond Mindfulness
By Charles Dray

I don't know how long I had been lying unconscious on the floor… It was 2008, and I had just experienced a Near Death Experience or NDE. I didn't know it then, but everything in my life was about to dramatically change.

In my mind, I drifted back to see the events of my life unfold as if I was watching a movie…seeing my childhood, which was spent traveling the world in a military family, and being exposed to many different people and cultures. We lived in places from Anchorage, Alaska to Naples, Italy and traveled extensively throughout Europe.

I experienced the devastating loss of my Father due to a plane crash when I was only 11 years old. During my subsequent rebellious teenage years during the late 60's and early 70's, "Sex, Drugs, and Rock-N-Roll" wasn't just a label; we lived it for better and for worse. But that's another story.

I dealt with the alcoholism of my step-father, a Marine Drill Instructor, by standing up to him when there were late night arguments between him and my mother, which usually ended up with me being knocked across the room.

By going to college, I got away from all the negativity and my former lifestyle. I immersed myself in my studies and new found love…martial arts!

Earning my Black Belt in Karate took five years of dedicated daily action and instilled the power and confidence that I could always draw upon in my life. In fact, I would apply many of the principles of the Martial Arts to my life and business, including focus, persistence, and the modeling of excellence.

It was through Karate training that I first learned about meditation, breathing skills, and sensory awareness. I learned skills to both harm and to heal. I studied Taoist practices and Tibetan Buddhism as I learned how to develop my personal skills and performance mindset to a very high degree.

After graduation from the University of Florida's College of Architecture, I spent years working in Sales and Business Development, ranging from Design/Build Construction and Real Estate Development, to working in Investment Banking and Insurance. I had a real passion for sales and working with people.

Early in my career I attended a summer program at Harvard Graduate School of Design for "Presentation Skills," where we used video footage to critique our work. The instructor was a professional in the television industry and taught me a number of skills and techniques for public speaking and sales. I've continued to use these tools and newer technologies to help others with public speaking and presentations.

All the training paid off as I took my first company from $700K in annual sales to over $4.3M annually in just a few short years. It was a busy time, as I was raising a family and was involved with my church and community.

Being an avid reader of self-development books, I learned about NLP in the early 1980's and had immediately put NLP to good use in developing rapport with my sales clients.

NLP is an acronym for Neuro-Linguistic Programming which was developed by Professor John Grinder and Richard Bandler. NLP is how we use the basic language of our mind to consistently achieve the results we want in life.

As the stock market crashed in 2008, and the U.S. economy imploded with banks no longer lending, my personal empire crashed down around me as well. I began to live the "Reverse American Dream" with a foreclosure, divorce, and the loss of my business. I knew firsthand what it meant to lose everything you had worked your entire life for…and I hit rock bottom!

Now on the night of my Near Death Experience, as I lay on the cold floor, covered in blood from a gash in my forehead, none of that mattered. I had entered into a time period that would be both my

"Dark Night of the Soul" on the material plane and my spiritual awakening on the inner plane.

What I felt through this NDE, however, was the deepest sense of love that I had ever felt in my life. Unconditional love supported me and was in virtually everything! I saw life differently as I watched the movie of my life unfold. I saw the life lessons and understood my path…my path of service to others.

"Start by doing what's necessary; then do what's possible; and suddenly you are doing the impossible." ~ St. Francis of Assisi

I took this quote to heart after my NDE and began focusing on what was in my control, which was my mindset and personal health. I also knew that a burning desire, hard work, and dedicated persistence would eventually pay off with the achievement of my goals, as it had during my previous years of sales and business success!

As I began working out daily at the gym, I changed my diet and modeled the training of local bodybuilders to achieve a total physical makeover in six months of dedicated training. This became the foundation of my future work as a trainer with functional fitness, nutrition, and holistic health.

During this physical transformation also came a deep spiritual healing as I sought out alternative and complementary healing methods.

Throughout this last decade, I've practiced yoga, deepened my meditation practice, and learned the techniques of everyday Mindfulness. I enjoy teaching Mindfulness techniques as they are very beneficial for stress reduction and helping to develop a serene inner calm amidst the chaos of life and business.

Going beyond Mindfulness, I became a Reiki Master Teacher and as a 4th generation Shihan, or teacher of Reiki, I help others learn this spiritual practice of self healing, restoring both physical and emotional well-being.

During this time, I also began cultivating my internal energy through the art of Chinese Qigong training, eventually becoming certified as an Instructor. Currently I am training in both South Mantis Kung Fu and Baguazhang.

Our bodies are meant to move, so discover your path, and dance, run, swim, or walk…connect to nature while you get out and move your body! Balancing the inner and the outer, Yin and Yang, the mental and the physical, is one of the secrets of leading an empowered life.

I love the interconnectedness of our natural world, our physical body, and consciousness! One of the modalities that I've become a facilitator of is "Access Consciousness Bars." Access Bars has assisted thousands of people to change many aspects of their lives. People report better health, ease of sleep, weight loss, better sex and relationships, relief from anxiety, and less stress.

My work as an Entrepreneur and Sales Consultant has regained a life of its own as I now connect with people on a much deeper level. At the same time, I pursued my passion for teaching, coaching, and hypnosis, earning my certification as a Clinical Hypnotherapist and Practitioner of NLP. I use these techniques and processes to deprogram the subconscious mind of limiting beliefs, then instill an upgrade to the mind's "software" for success and abundance.

Now as a certified Life and Success Coach, I'm able to draw on these life experiences, lessons, and tools to help transform my client's lives and businesses, as they become empowered to live the life of their dreams.

I am a Changemaker… What's your dream?

Charles Dray, C.Ht., is an Enlightened Entrepreneur, Life and Success Coach.

He is a Clinical Hypnotherapist, Certified Practitioner of NLP and an Access Consciousness Bars Facilitator. His coaching practice focuses on helping clients through Personal Breakthrough Sessions to achieve Excellence and Success in both business and life.

To find out more about Charles and his work visit: www.thrivealignment.com

This is the Time!
By Dorothy-Inez Del Tufo

Do you have a dream still left inside of you? Do you wonder what your life would've been like if you had tried to live it out? Well, that was how I felt ten short years ago.

It's hard to believe it's been that long since I decided to leave my high-paying corporate job to pursue my dream of being a makeup artist. As a teenager, I always wanted to be in the music industry as a singer or dancer. I was never encouraged to pursue those dreams because my father was concerned that there was too much competition and that I would not make any money in that field.

My biggest dream was to be on stage with Prince, singing and dancing. I didn't believe that dream was possible, so being a makeup artist became my back up plan. My thought was that if I became Prince's makeup artist, I would create an opportunity to sing for him and he would ask me to join his group. Sounds like a pretty good plan, right? Wrong!

Like many, I got caught up in my parent's vision for me. I slowly let my artistic abilities die and began to focus on a "real" career as a secretary. Do you remember that term? Now, they are called administrative assistants. I did that work for years in Germany, which is where I was born and raised. Who knew that as a secretary my dream would partially come true? I was blessed to go on two tours with Prince, thanks to my friend, Boni Boyer, who was his keyboardist at the time. I did not get to be his makeup artist, nor did I get discovered, but I had the privilege of being backstage and at all the after-parties for two of his European tours.

Do you want to know how that came to be? Getting the opportunity to experience being backstage and that close to Prince happened because I was persistent and focused on what I wanted. I met Boni on one of his earlier tours while sitting in the lobby of his hotel hoping to meet someone who could get me up close and personal. Yes, I was otherwise known as a groupie.

Boni and I hit it off and soon became like sisters. Whenever they came to Germany on tour I was one of the first people she called. I make my dreams come true by being focused on the outcome and doing what it takes to make it happen, like meeting and being close to Prince. I've met so many celebrities this way. I often wonder what could have happened if I had let Boni know exactly what I wanted - to sing and dance for Prince, and that I had a whole book of songs I wrote for him to see. But at the end of the day I desired an authentic relationship with her and didn't want her to feel used, so I kept my focus on our friendship instead of using her to meet Prince. Now that they are both gone I often wish I had been more forthright.

The lesson we can learn is that we can't assume we have time to play with our dreams, because we never know what's going to happen, so we must seize the opportunity when it arises. I thought I would have time later to tell her my dream of singing and dancing with Prince as our friendship developed. But as fate would have it, Boni died three years after we met, and as we all know, Prince too is now gone.

Why are you waiting? What is keeping you from stepping into your dream? Are you afraid to ask for what you want? Is someone telling you that you're too old? I'm here to tell you it's never too late!

When I worked as a manager at T-mobile, I would play a VHS tape from motivational speaker Les Brown called, "This is Your Decade," for all my new employees. My goal was to inspire them to be the best they could be, whether it was at my company or another. I have always loved developing outstanding leaders.

The funny thing was that I never considered that message for myself until one day in 2004. I accidentally found out that a young, white male, with six years less experience, was making $7000 more per year than I was for the same job. I took my issue to human resources, and of course I had no success with them. I contemplated on what to do, and Les' message came to mind again. I decided, "This **will** be my decade!" I began to plan the exit from my job. I got accepted at the top makeup school in Los Angeles, so I took a leave of absence to move closer to my dream.

Two years later, at the age of 40, I graduated from college with a

Bachelors in Communications, all paid for by the company I was leaving! I had worked on that degree since I was 30, and committed to myself that I would finish by the time I was 40. It wasn't easy but it was one of my proudest moments.

I graduated at the top of my class and received a special award for Educational Perseverance, because while in school, my husband was stationed in Biloxi, Mississippi and only a month after living there, we lost everything to Hurricane Katrina. It was the most devastating times of my life, yet I maintained a high level of performance through it all. Then, one week after I graduated, I submitted my two-week notice and began my journey as an entrepreneur.

Being an entrepreneur has been one of the most enriching experiences of my life. I have grown as a leader and most of all as a woman. Who knew that one could experience new-found success at the age of 40? I started my business, being known as the Minister of Beauty, because I used the first part of my own journey to self love, and my gifts in beauty to empower other women to own who they are inside and out. It is out of our own journey that God births something beautiful, and He turns our mess into our message.

Trust me when I tell you nothing is happening *to* you, everything is happening *for* you. It is all preparation for your destination. When you can begin to see and believe that truth, your whole world will transform. You will begin to see things through a different lens, which removes a lot of stress that comes from negative thinking. Everything that has ever happened in your past, present, and future makes you the person God needs you to be to carry out the mission you were sent here to accomplish.

More recently, in 2014, my husband was unexpectedly laid off from the military. My business was on the rise. I was becoming well-known in the coaching world; I had just become an International Best-Selling author and speaker in Seattle. Then, once again my world began tumbling down. I went from living in a 3000 square-foot home to an 800 square-foot apartment, literally overnight. The army released us from the military, so my landlord quickly allowed us to move into the smaller home he was staying in so we could afford the rent. My husband went through a deep depression which put a tremendous strain on our marriage.

I had to figure out a way to bring in more money because he wasn't working. His layoff is what led me to pursuing the next goal that I had put off; a Masters degree. As a military spouse, the G.I. Bill pays me to go to school, so it was the perfect solution. I used that money to sustain me and my business as I continued to grow and develop. I have to admit, it still wasn't easy because of the emotional stress I dealt with at home.

Then another disruption came in the middle of working on my degree. We had to decide where we wanted to make our final move with the army. We could choose to move anywhere in the world as our final destination. My husband didn't want to stay in Seattle which is where we were stationed, so I meditated for a while, because he left the decision of where to live up to me.

I thought back to my childhood dream of living in Hollywood and being star. I always told my husband that when I died I wanted my ashes to be sprinkled in the California ocean. Forget going there when I died, NOW was my chance to live there and see if I could make it as a makeup artist. But God had other plans for me.

Once again, I found myself reflecting on Les Brown's message saying, "The richest place on the planet is the graveyard because so many people died with their dreams and inventions still left inside of them." The truth is most of us have fewer years in front of us than we do behind. At this point in my life I'm so committed to living with no regrets that I decided to relocate to California. When it came time to locate a new school to finish my degree, God told me to look up "Bible colleges in Los Angeles."

If I can be honest, I did not want to attend a Bible college, as I have an aversion to religiosity, but in the spirit of obedience, I Googled them and found the Bible Institute of Los Angeles, also known as BIOLA. I have to say I was floored because God gave me the name of that school when he spoke it to my spirit in His still, small voice. It just happens to be one of the top seminaries in the country.

The school required a lot to be accepted, and by the grace of God I got in with no ministry background at all. Unfortunately that school did not work out, but I believe God sent me there for a season to learn what I need to know about what Christian women were directly dealing with concerning empowerment. I ended up finding the right school, and I reached my final destination of becoming an Organizational Psychologist.

So this new decade has started off right! At the age of 50, I have walked on fire with Tony Robbins, become a four-time International Best-Selling author, Speaker, and Organizational Psychologist. I also re-launched a new business in California as a Confidence and Personal Presence coach, helping high-achieving women like me have the courage to grow and step into their dreams. It's been a beautiful journey. If I can do this, so can you!

This is not the time to play small; this is the time to play big! This is the time to take risks and make things happen! This is the time to no longer care what others say about you! This is the time to be the person God has called you to be! This is the time to create a legacy so the world knows you were here!

Dorothy-Inez, not Dorothy, is a four-time International Best-Selling Author, Speaker, and Coach for high achieving women in transition who want to show up with more purpose, power, and presence in their personal and professional lives.

She holds a Bachelors of Science in Communications and a Master's of Science in Organizational Psychology. She has a passion for God, spirituality, and Prince. She lives in the Los Angeles area with her two poodles Snuggles and Jazmin.

Connect with her at www.dorothyinez.com or www.facebook.com/dorothyinez

Stop Holding Yourself Hostage To The Past!
By Delia Joseph

What's holding you back? And how do you free yourself from the past?

Do you feel like you're standing still?
Not sure where you are going?
Or how you are going to get there?

The first step to finally breaking free and embracing your unique power and beauty begins with recognizing that **YOU** are **"Valuable by Design™."**

Valuable: having admirable or esteemed characteristics

Design: an artist or fashion plan or blueprint.

Knowing that you are **Valuable by Design** means you possess the skills, the ability, and the talent to create whatever it is you truly believe for yourself. YOU choose what you desire to bring into your life, and what you desire to remove and release.

Knowing that you are **Valuable by Design** begins with a clear understanding of what brings you joy into your life: an inventory of the people, places, things, thoughts, and ideas that light you up. Bringing joy into your life all starts with an Understanding of Self. It's through this joy that you will experience personal success. You don't experience the joy once you get what you desire; you get what you desire because you are joyful.

I wasn't always clear on who I was, where I was going in life, or that I possessed the power to create and call in whatever it was I desired.

I was sexually abused at very young age before my family moved to Canada. Imagine a young black girl at five-years old with a heavy British accent, who suddenly finds herself in Canada in the 1960s. I lived in the central part of the City where no one looked like me and

I was made to feel insignificant by the community, my neighbours, teachers, and classmates.

As a result, I felt broken growing up; I lacked confidence, self-worth, and was insecure. I found myself identifying and viewing the world heavily through the lens of my past. The things that happened to me as a child brought me pain, anxiety, stress, and anger as I grew up.

As far as I knew, I was the only person that had been sexually abused at the age of two. I lost my faith and trust in God. I didn't like going to church because I couldn't understand how an all-mighty God could let this happen to a child – to me.

As I got older, I was sick and tired of being sick and tired from giving my power away. Tired of holding on to the negative BS (belief system). I had this yearning that there was more inside of me but I did not know what.

I questioned life. Why am I here? Why did all those ugly circumstances happen to me?

I finally realized I was holding myself hostage by replaying past hurts that did not actually occur in the present. By keeping myself hostage I robbed myself of special moments; the story that replayed in my mind stole my joy, affected my immune system, caused illnesses, pain, and migraines, and impacted meaningful relationships.

Eventually, I found the courage to reclaim my relationship with God – and I also had to establish a relationship with myself. I had to work hard, really, really hard at loving myself, at allowing myself to be loved. By me. By others. By life.

That is when I found my worth.

The steps I took to find my worth were to:

1. Forgive myself and forgive others.
2. Let go of the things that no longer serve me.

3. Believe in myself by using my words to create not to destroy.
4. Consistently create a daily habit.

I started seeing value in myself, my surroundings, and in others. I valued myself and started associating with people I could learn from. I went back to school to expand my knowledge (because knowledge is power), and took Business Management courses.

In various positions that I worked, I was introduced to mediation. I then developed an interest in the process of mediation. Mediation helped further my understanding of my self-worth and the self-worth of others. I made a lot of assumptions about myself and my relationships with others. I realized I didn't have to stay in conflict with myself or my relationships with others.

I came across a book called, *The 4 Agreements,* by Don Miquel Ruiz.

In the book there are four agreements that each person makes within:

1. Be impeccable with your word.
2. Don't take anything personally.
3. Don't make assumptions.
4. Always do your best.

These agreements changed my perspective of how I saw myself and others!

How? By having the courage to ask myself questions and being honest with my answers.

How? By having the courage to ask others questions and not make assumptions.

And the journey didn't end there.

Letting go was not easy. I had to DECIDE and COMMIT to letting go; I had to have a strong desire to change, so much that I could feel it in my body, my spirit, and my bones.

I had to make a decision to let go of thoughts, words, and behavior that no longer served me.

Buh-bye to, "I can't." Buh-bye to, "I shouldn't." Buh-bye to, "I don't know."

Because the words that follow "I" and "I am" become your reality.

As a result of an exercise that I learned from one of my mentors, I learned that you have to manage your thoughts and behaviours, and choose your words carefully; don't let your thoughts manage you. Managing my thoughts, behaviours, and words eventually became natural, and engaging with the world became a joyful experience. What made this exercise a game-changer was the freedom to choose whether or not to address people and issues face to face. Either way, I was able to release the icky, negative energy from my system, and not hold on to it anymore. By doing this I set myself free. And in the process I also realized that by letting go I am not saying, "It's okay that the abuse happened," I am saying "**I LOVE MYSELF** enough to no longer live in pain."

Say it with me: "**I LOVE MYSELF** enough to no longer live in pain."

Here are the steps of the exercise I used:

1. **First find a safe space where you are not going to be disturbed or distracted.**
2. **Have a pen and paper. Also have some hot lemon water or plain water.**
3. **Make sure you have a full length mirror.**
4. **Sit on the floor in front of the mirror. By doing this you're grounding yourself.**
5. **Make yourself comfortable and start writing out the issues/problems.**
6. **After writing, look at yourself in the mirror and forgive yourself for holding on to the pain of the past.**

When I did this exercise I really needed to let go of the abuse that took place when I was young. I wrote out how I truly felt; the pain that it caused me, and the people I blamed for not protecting me. I had to forgive myself for holding onto the past, because, in reality, the abuse was no longer happening. But the memories were so painful, I felt like I would not be here if my parents had not moved to another country. The exercise helped me realize the very people that I had blamed for not protecting me saved my life. Had I not taken the steps to let go I would never have come to this realization and been able to forgive.

After writing out my thoughts and pain, I burned the letter and slowly released my anger. I replaced this letter with a new letter of how I desire to feel and then wrote it out in the present tense, because what you focus on expands. Focusing on the positive helped to heal me. Over time I got fewer and fewer migraines. I started to see myself and love myself. As I respected myself I then respected others. I started taking responsibility for my thoughts and actions.

I slowly started believing in myself and having confidence by using my words to create and not to destroy. I learned about self talk and how believing what others say can cause a negative effect. For example if someone said that "You are not smart," I would then say it to myself over and over until I began to really believe it. T.D. Jakes said,

"It's not what others say about **YOU** that determines your destiny it is what you say about **YOU**."

The more I spoke against myself the more it became my reality and I could not figure out why that was. Until I learned that **WORDS** have power!

I began to speak about how smart and intelligent I was; I started believing in myself, seeing myself as valuable.

I enrolled in college to take a two-year Business Management course. By the last course I ended up with an A! What a shock! I had never made an A on my report card. By determination and belief in myself, I was able to accomplish the goal I set out.

Along my journey, I developed a routine that would help me show gratitude that looks like this:

1. **I say, "Good Morning God." "Good Morning Delia." "Good Morning World."**
2. **I give praise and glory to God and thank Him for breathing life into me.**
3. **I meditate for five minutes (you can find YouTube videos to teach you).**
4. **I exercise for five to ten minutes.**

These steps actually help you get unstuck so you stop holding yourself hostage to the past.

Having a coach/accountability partner was essential to my success. I would not be where I am now without mentors, coaches, and the people I would surround myself with who challenged me to want better for myself.

As I started to live my life on purpose and find more meaning in my life, I became calmer, more self-aware, and more confident.

I started attracting people who were seeking to move beyond the very thing I healed myself from – Holding Myself Hostage to the Past.

I now teach people how to get out of their own way.

In order to do that you have to address what is in front of you or inside of you, and be willing to make the shift to improve your life. Understand that growth (i.e. life) is a continual process. Yes! It is a matter of choice to see your life through a different perspective. It's about getting rid of the judgment you placed on yourself and others. This new perspective is about finding your **GREATNESS**! This is why I call myself an Improveologist!

It's time.
Get to know YOU.
Celebrate yourself.
Invest in YOU.

Born in England, raised in Canada, Delia Joseph has worked more than 25 years with people in different capacities. She is a Certified Mediator, Certified Professional Life Coach, and has her own practice: Improveology Lifestyle Coaching.

Even though some parts of her life were traumatic which lead to some unhealthy life decisions, that did not stop her from wanting the best for herself and others. She pursued a career in mediation, life coaching, mentoring, and facilitating to help others get unstuck.

Delia has developed and facilitated workshops at the Victim Offender Mediation Association conference in Philadelphia, PA. Closer to home, she has facilitated victim sensitivity workshops for the Justice Committee, as well as regularly facilitated "Colour of Fear," a full-day workshop addressing racism. She has been featured on several occasions as a Guest Speaker at the Congress of Black Women and the Jamaican Association.

Delia works with Mid-Life Transitioners, who are frustrated, stressed, or unhappy to eliminate and delete thoughts and habits that no longer serve them so they can live a healthier and fulfilled lifestyle.

Click here www.improveologylifestylecoaching.com to schedule a Soulful Conversation with Improveologist Delia Joseph!

How I Became a Solutionista
By Trudy Miller

I love helping people get exactly what they want - and even more than they imagined they could possibly have. I love watching them squeal with delight once our work/playtime together is done. I get squealers from all sectors of life, because I've traveled many pathways to arrive at my calling.

At age nine, I was already an artist, idea explorer, and problem solver. My parents were extremely supportive in allowing me to pursue many interests. My fashionista mom encouraged me to design clothes and get them made by a local seamstress. My dad engaged me in making art, playing with his mechanical drawing tools, and I was very curious about the way things worked.

I looked forward to the weekends. That's when I got to learn macramé, batik, tie dye, and visit Dolly the seamstress with my mom, or go to the art store and museums with my dad. When I wasn't doing any of those things, I was playing with Legos, Barbies, and solving 3D puzzles.

My interest in art, visual patterns, nature, and numbers drew me to the work of Leonardo da Vinci - initially via Disney. Leonardo made sculptures, designed buildings, and invented contraptions for a living. I too wanted to be an Artist-Engineer. When I had this conversation with my Dad, he explained that at that time (the late 70's) people had to choose one profession. He had also wanted to be an artist while growing up, but he explained that the path of an artist was difficult, so I should find a way to be useful and creative in the areas of food, clothing, or shelter. In his case, he chose textile design and engineering, and did art on the side.

Our home was also being renovated at the time and I became extremely fascinated with architecture. It was the ultimate 3D puzzle. My Dad designed the improvements with a local builder, and he included me in all the design meetings. It was then that I decided I would study architecture first, and work my way back into my other interests. I never explained this to my family because it sounded too complicated, and I had no idea how I was going to do it

- or why I didn't want to choose just one career. All I knew at the time was that if I could learn to design buildings, I could do anything.

The grades I got in high school did not reflect my abilities, however. My art teachers weren't fond of my work, and I wasn't great at math. Fortunately, my parents were still encouraging, and they reminded me that my graduating grades would come from independent evaluators in another country. That meant everything to me, because it kept me confident in my creative abilities - despite my average grades.

Much later on, I discerned I was slightly dyslexic, and I'm pretty sure I would have been diagnosed with inattentive ADHD (quiet daydreamer; easily bored or distracted, hyperactive brain) if that was 'a thing' when I was in high school. Years later, my learning challenges have become my superpowers in the realm of problem solving. I became really good at algebra, and found I was very comfortable with identifying and solving for X in almost any situation.

I used my hyper-focusing abilities to create my own systems, tools, and methods for navigating the world around me, because I found that I was really good at doing complex things, but I had a harder time with what seemed elementary to most people. I was often very frustrated by these challenges in college and grad school. My mother comforted me when I was sobbing about being unable to remember things, being unable to concentrate, or being unable to wake up in the morning. She always reminded me that there were lots of things I could do that others found really difficult, and she always had great suggestions about how to manage my time and my memory.

I was often ashamed and anxious about not remembering things, or misreading instructions, so I started creating charts and diagrams for everything I heard so I could process the information visually, just like I did in architecture school. Things improved for me, and I found that the charts and diagrams were also useful for connecting new dots and generating new ideas. My tools emboldened me to devise new methods of doing things in ways that supported how I experienced the world. I became the goldilocks of everything, and started designing things that felt "just right" for the way I saw the world. It was then that I realized I needed a new title. One of my interns summed me up with *Solutionista*, and it felt just right.

About ten years ago, I started designing clothes because I was tired of feeling badly about my body after I left a fitting room, and I was utterly fed up with what was happening in fashion. Everywhere I looked, I was greeted by a muffin top or butt-crack. My battle cry of "I'm not fucking doing that!" resulted in a line of timeless silhouettes that accommodated the full range of body cycles women experience over time - including puberty, pregnancy, weight fluctuation, and menopause.

The method I employed to develop the clothing line was a direct result of my architectural training and interest in sustainable design. However, the reason I felt drawn to design clothing in first place had more to do with how I felt about my body. I also knew I was not alone. In fact, 94% of women think something is wrong with their bodies, and that has a profound impact on the way they show up in the world.

The goldilocks in me knew there was another way to design and fabricate clothes that made women of all shapes and sizes look and feel great about themselves - with more ease, comfort, and fluidity. What I didn't know at the time was that the fashion industry did not share the same vision or aspirations back then - or that there would be such intense negative pushback. Everything I did went against the grain of an industry I only became familiar with because I needed things to be very different than they were. I was an outsider - challenging fast fashion with timeless design, embracing plus-sized women in my marketing, using my customers instead of professional models, etc.

Though my work was well received by my customers, I did not make fashion industry inroads. The whole concept was way more disruptive than I initially thought. My retail store crashed and burned a year after the market collapse of 2008, and I was forced to put the line in the freezer so I could recover and regroup. I was burned out, because I still worked full-time as an architect, with seven-day workweeks. I stopped traveling, practicing yoga, making time for friends and family, and doing everything I found pleasurable for the sake of the clothing line - and that clearly wasn't working out for me. It was time to turn my *Solutionista* lenses on myself.

It was on that rehabilitation journey that it became clear to me that my work was more about wellness and beauty than fashion. The clothes are like makeup for women's bodies, framing their best features, and downplaying perceived flaws.

It also became clear that my inclusive and body positive message resonated strongly with *Solutionistas* who were also on wellness journeys. Over the past ten years, I discovered I had healing abilities around body image that are independent of my designs. This insight led me to create workshops and individual experiences designed to shift the way women saw themselves, and it has become such an incredible source of joy and pleasure for me. And to top it off, now I only sell my clothes at wellness events, or wellness facilities I've had the privilege of designing.

For many years, I couldn't imagine giving up my identity as an architect or academic to be a clothing designer, because I was not in full acknowledgement or appreciation of how important beauty is to us as human beings. Now I live to light women up with the glow of their own beauty. I get to see and hear them squeal with delight within five minutes of our being together. As an architect, I still have to wait several months or sometimes years to get that feedback!

This work has also freed me up to appreciate my own beauty, which was an unexpected bonus. I often deflected compliments on my attractiveness, opting to identify as smart and useful rather than soft and beautiful. I constantly tried to prove that I wasn't just another pretty face, which created a life of overwork and overwhelm for myself that I could not move beyond. Now I'm a proud purveyor of smart, useful, soft, hyper-functional and beautiful empowerment tools that change people's lives for the better - and I couldn't be happier or more proud.

Trudy Miller is a Jamaican-born architect, designer, and creative strategy consultant, practicing what she calls *juicy minimalism.* Her "Whole Systems" approach to design - from fashion to furniture - is all about doing more with less in comfort, ease, and style. Trudy earned her stripes as a clothing designer and body image expert when she created a line of convertible clothing designed to accommodate the full range of body cycles women experience over time - including puberty, pregnancy, weight fluctuation, and menopause .

Miller has taught at some of the country's top design schools, and her press highlights include television features on NBC's Today Show and BRIC TV. Magazine features include Inc., Time Out, Essence, Vice, and Heart & Soul Magazine.

To learn more about Trudy, visit www.solutionista.com

The Power of Small Things!
By Sherrod C. Schuler

From early on, while growing up in the city of Flint, MI, I always knew I wanted to do something big. In fact, I would spend hours in my parent's basement dreaming of being something special. Whether it was dribbling my favorite basketball, rapping lyrics to the latest rap song, or performing a presidential address to an audience of no one. I felt I was created to do something great!

Eventually, like most inner-city youth, I created a Plan A to become an NBA basketball star. However, this dream slowly faded away when I realized the cold, hard reality that I wasn't growing any taller than 5'7", not to mention that my skills were rather average. At least this is what I concluded quickly when I competed against guys in my hometown who would later go on to play for major college programs and the NBA. I was definitely out of my league.

This failed dream wouldn't stop me from pursuing my Plan B - to get a college degree. I wanted to go to one of those big-name universities, but I settled on a smaller school in West Michigan called Grand Valley State University. As it turned out, it was a good choice. Go Lakers!

After graduation in four years, I couldn't wait to get to the big city! All my hard work was going to pay off and I was finally going to contribute something back into the world. I just knew I was going to get this great marketing job working for one of the big three automakers or a big-name industry. I applied and applied to get hired by one those companies only to be rejected several times.

Reluctantly, I started a career in banking. I enjoyed the banking world so much so, that I lasted in that industry for over 10 years. It must have been all the wonderful people that I met throughout the years that kept me there. I mostly enjoyed the coaching and motivating aspect of my job. As the manager, my job was to help others perform and achieve their best results.

Then, all of a sudden, as the company began to focus its attention on migrating customers to more digital transactions, it hit me. Although I liked my job, my personal career had not progressed and my comfort zone was beginning to feel disrupted. I began to feel lost and trapped. Something was nudging me. What was my purpose in life? Had I missed my destiny altogether? I thought to myself, "All the big things I wanted to do in life never seemed to work out, so just calm down." I convinced myself to relax and to ignore the voice inside.

This thought haunted me and kept me feeling stuck. I couldn't seem to move forward anymore. It was as if I could see what I desired to be doing, but the dream seemed to be too great to obtain. There were times that I wanted to go after that big promotion or start my own business, but I would pull back the moment I felt resistance. I came to a place where I did not want to be disappointed anymore.

Then, I heard about a motivational speaker from YouTube who was going to give a series of speeches at the urban shoe store close to my branch. I was curious and began to investigate who this guy was. The event was free and he would give a weekly inspirational speech open to the public. I decided to test my curiosity and show up to the event, not knowing anyone there. I definitely had my skeptical radar on.

When I arrived, there were about 30 to 40 people present. I said to myself, "Yeah, this is just some publicity stunt." I was shocked to see that he was performing a speech in a small room filled with kids and a few adults. My initial thought was, "Why is he giving speeches at the local shoe store? Isn't he 'big time?'"

I must admit this experience wasn't a high-profile event, but as I stood there, I watched the huge impact he had on those who came to listen. I thought to myself, "Why aren't the news reporters reporting this? This is some good stuff." In his presentation he spoke to those kids as if he was in a room filled with thousands of people. It was in that very moment that I realized the true power of what was happening before my eyes. I was witnessing how to achieve big things by doing the little things just as hard. Then, intensely he shouted out to the small group, "You are not average; stop acting like it!" In those few words, it was as if something beyond him was talking to me personally. This became my "ah-ha" moment.

His message ignited the fire from within regarding my passion. The feeling was very familiar with the type of work ethic I was accustomed to. In addition to him perfecting his craft in speaking, he was there to give his gift back those who were in the room. You see while growing up in Flint, I saw this type of selfless act, determination, and tenacity from many people all around me. It was as if there was something in the water that made those I was around do great things.

For instance, my father was an example as I watched him work long, hard hours every day, because he was committed to ensuring his three children obtained their college degrees debt-free. You see, he had decided that he would sacrifice pursuing his career ambitiously, to ensure his children achieved their goals.

Or maybe it was my high-school basketball coach, who pushed our team in practice, doing conditioning drills every day, which led us to achieve our dream of winning a state championship, even though there wasn't much money involved for him.

Perhaps it was the pastor from my hometown of Flint who stepped out on faith and started a small congregation, while still working a full-time job, which ultimately led me to accept Christ.

It was in these life lessons I had while growing up that I was reminded that doing the little things consistently will ultimately lead to something great. In other words, my mission in life to empower others is to never give up and to keep pushing forward. Contrary, to the many misconceptions about people from my hometown, I witnessed hard work in action every day as a child that shaped who I am today. It was these little lessons and many others that gave me the example to know that dreams can be achieved when there is a commitment to a series of small things.

After my encounter with this motivational speaker, I realized it was not the big stage, the lights, the cameras, or the televised program that were going to make the difference in these children's future. It was the fact that he was showing up to pour life lessons into their lives. I knew from that moment of realization my voice to speak life to others had to be my "why" to go forward in everything that I do. Before this moment, I felt everything needed to be big or it didn't have much merit. This quickly helped me see that my perception of a big event was a false illusion. Sometimes all you have to do is show up to make a difference. You never know whose life you will inspire in the process.

Therefore, I had an obligation to all those leaders in the past and present that were committed to seeing me grow as a person. I had to pay it forward with the same passion, regardless if I thought my message was big or not. In fact, I owed it to God and myself to serve the world. Therefore, I decided to move forward and stop waiting on something major to happen to pursue my goals. So, why I am sharing my story? Honestly, I never considered myself to be much of a writer, but I must share this story to inspire others to reach for their dreams.

It has become my assignment to help as many people as I can see how they can live the life they are destined to have so they can further help others. I decided I wanted to help people break free from insecurities, fears, confusion, and the thoughts of feeling insignificant that keep them stuck, and to rediscover the path God created for them. My job is to show up and pour out what has been invested in me. No matter what the setback or obstacle is, I am convinced that all things can work together for your good. It has become my belief: *It is happening as we speak!*

Sherrod Schuler is a poised, polished, and articulate speaker, presenter of ideas, and a leader. He is an accomplished management professional with significant achievements in the financial services industry. Sherrod is an ordained minister with the Jabula New Life International Network and an Associate Pastor of Embassy Covenant Church International of Troy, MI. He received his bachelor's degree from Grand Valley State University in Marketing and holds an MBA from Spring Arbor University. Sherrod resides in the Metro Detroit area with his wife, Bridgette Schuler. He is the proud father of one daughter, Autumn.

To learn more visit: www.sherrodschuler.com
Or email at sherrodschuler@yahoo.com

Now is the Time
By Shauna-Kaye Brown

"Transformation is a process, and as life happens there are tons of ups and downs. It's a journey of discovery - there are moments on mountaintops and moments in deep valleys of despair." – **Rick Warren**

May 2016, marked a turning point in my life. For the first time ever, I was fired from a job. I felt like my life could not have gotten any worse. As you might guess, I was completely devastated. Imagine being away from your family, in a different country, and suddenly told that you no longer have a job! Of course, I did not know then what a blessing that would be.

As we often do when we become destitute, I questioned God, wanting to know, *"why me?"* It is interesting how self-centered we become when we experience dire circumstances. We tend to believe that it's all about us. It was not until that cataclysmic event occurred that I realized how much my momentum had slowed. In fact, I felt completely immobilized.

The reality is I had felt stuck for at least two years prior to becoming jobless, hopeless, and fearful. Nothing I did seemed to help eliminate that feeling of complete stagnation. As if that was not bad enough, now I had bills to pay, I was in a foreign land, I had no job, and the one person I felt cared had walked away. So of course, I questioned God. After all wasn't He the author and finisher of everything? So, why did He abandon me?

Yet, out of disappointment comes enlightenment. About two months after losing my job, in this moment of hurt and loss, I started going to church. During this season, the theme at church was, *'We Are More than Conquerors.'* The focus was on Romans, chapter **8**, and I was particularly taken with verse 28. *"And we know that all things work together for good to them that love God, to them who are the called according to His* purpose."

It was then that the Universe gave me the chance of a lifetime, the opportunity to find and live my purpose. God came through for me in a way that I had never experienced before. Don't get me wrong, I have always believed in God, but this occurrence renewed my hope and catapulted me into a new understanding of what it means to leave it all up to Him. After just two months of losing my job, I found a new one, and I was tasked with meaningfully helping people. Not only did I find a better job, it was one that was completely aligned with my purpose.

I had not always doubted God's plan for my life. As a child, I had complete faith in God and I did not think anything was impossible. I had many book characters through whom I lived vicariously, and I knew one day what I imagined would become my reality. Yet, after being knocked down too many times, you find yourself believing that's the way life is.

The experience of being knocked down by life reminds me of my last year in high school. It was filled with so much uncertainty because my mother told me that after high school, she was done with helping me financially. My hopes were dashed; I had big dreams of continuing my education. Hence, my mother's decree made things very complicated and I started to experience the onset of hopelessness and helplessness. My mind often wandered to all the prior moments when I had been knocked down.

The Early Years

The life I lived growing up and the one I dreamed of were at best paradoxical. I was born in a one-bedroom government house in rural Jamaica, where I spent all my childhood. I grew up with six siblings, five of whom lived with my mother and me in that one bedroom. I stayed there until I was sixteen years old, after which I left home. Life was hard growing up, but I did life hard because I had no choice.

I started reading at two years old, and by the age of ten I read all the books my mother stored on her three makeshift bookshelves. Little did I know then, that being such an avid reader would open my mind to unknown realities and would evoke an undying longing inside of me. I knew then that I wanted to be somebody. I wanted to be affluent and to live like the ladies in my novels. I admired **Maya Angelou** and I went around reciting *Phenomenal Woman* every chance I got. I believed I was phenomenal! I was very diligent and persistent, and education was very important to me. More than anything, I wanted to help people, so I had to become a success.

My reality then was abject poverty, but my dream was affluence and philanthropy. I knew I wanted to help people, especially people like me. My decision solidified when at the age of twelve I was stopped dead in my tracks by someone much stronger than me. I went through an ordeal that resulted in a drastic change in who I was and what I thought I could do, what I thought I could be. After that traumatic experience, I lost my confidence, hope, trust, and belief in humanity. I became very reserved and only found solace in the myriad of books I read. But one thing that did not die was my zeal to succeed; if anything, I became more determined than ever before.

You see, I blamed what happened to me on my circumstances. I thought, "If we weren't poor, this would not have happened." After that, I made a pact with myself to get out of poverty. Education was my outlet. I knew I wanted to help people and I could not let what happened to me, happen to anyone else, if I could help it. There is something extremely debilitating about poverty that gets into your head and immobilizes you. If you are not mentally tough, you can sink under the pressure at the drop of a hat. It did not help that I was completely clueless at the time. However, I continued to believe success was possible, no matter what. If others could do it, so could I.

Believe and Grow

During my final year of high school, while performing mandatory community service at a law firm, I told the lawyer who ran the firm about my dream to attend the University of the West Indies, the top-ranked university in Jamaica at the time. He quickly told me to be more realistic. It was not likely that I would make it to that institution coming from my high school, he exclaimed. He told me that I was aiming too high and my dreams would be dashed if I did not change that wishful thought. What saved me from his myopic mental purview was my will to win and my abhorrence for poverty.

What he did not know was that my determination was greater than my fears, that going to university was not a destination for me but a route. I had big dreams, and like my mother instilled in me from the outset, education was the only way. I believed this completely. I had dreams of one day owning a home with detailed stone work and a long drive way, of building my mother a home of her own, and leaving a life of poverty. I needed to attend university and no one was going to tell me differently. The expression, *"stand up for what you believe in,"* suddenly had meaning for me. There is a marked difference between just saying something and believing what you are saying. A new fire ignited in me then, and I was determined more than ever to keep it alight.

Unfortunately, upon graduation, my parents could not afford to send me to college so I joined the National Youth Service Corps. I worked for a year and received a stipend which amounted to a paltry sum at best. The following year I went to college even though I had no money to pay the tuition. Many doors were opened and closed before me during this time. But in these lean years, I learned how to survive by working while attending school. I perfected the art of dedication and got accustomed to asking for what I wanted. I asked, believing I would receive, and in many instances I did. I understood that hearing '*no*' was not the end of the world but a closer proximity to hearing '*yes*.'

So, it should come as no surprise that, after college I was accepted into the University of the West Indies and graduated three years later with a Bachelor of Science Degree. You see, my mother had already planted the seeds of success in my mind. These seeds were watered by determination and persistence. If you don't defy the laws of nature, your results will be favorable. So, while many thought my desires were impossible dreams, I knew they were a natural progression. One of the things I learned during those years is that the mind is more powerful than we can ever begin to imagine. *Through faith, hard work, and an inherent will to win, my dream became a reality*. This statement is my mandate and I am sticking to it!

Purpose on the Heels of Frustration

Though I knew then that I had the desire to help others, not knowing how I would be able to help meant putting this desire off until the opportune time. Meanwhile, life happened. My mother's cardinal rule to 'get an education' was forever etched in my mind and was paramount for me. It meant that, all my life until I was twenty-eight years old, I attended school. I acquired multiple degrees, attended law school, became an Attorney-at-Law, and in 2014, decided that it was time to make a life for myself. I was excited about undertaking legal practice. By then, I had sent out about fifty job applications, and eagerly anticipated the myriad of job offers from which I would have to choose one.

But why, after these major accomplishments, did I feel so unfulfilled and perpetually stuck? More so, was there a logical explanation for me to feel like a failure? My emotional state successfully defied logic, it was as if I had failed miserably. Worse yet, I felt completely alone. At one point, I had a committed partner who did everything in his power to ensure I had what I needed, but the gnawing anxiety persisted. For two long years, I only existed. Rather than truly living, I was slowly dying.

So, when I was called in by my boss that fateful day in May 2016, the Universe had a plan, though I didn't know it then. When I say being fired was a blessing, understand that I needed to be stopped, I needed to be awakened. Suddenly, like an epiphany I understood the longing I had experienced for so many years. It dawned on me that, you can accomplish everything that others think is amazing, but if you are not living *your* purpose, it means nothing. Others constantly told me how accomplished I was, but none of those accolades excited me the way finding my calling did. Having a job that allows me to meaningfully help people is both rewarding and fulfilling.

Today, I am immensely grateful for that frightful day I lost my job, as it was then that I found myself.

Shauna-kaye L. Brown is a multifaceted budding entrepreneur whose main focus is to assist individuals to manifest their greatness. She runs an insightful, content-rich blog at www.shauna-kayelbrown.com and has a visible presence on social media where she shares daily insights and encouragement. She is an outstanding Motivational Speaker who has spoken at various places such as the Brown Memorial Baptist Church and the Langston Hughes Senior Center both in Brooklyn, New York.

Shauna-kaye is keen on helping people and has participated in a myriad of projects geared toward personal growth and development. She is an astute motivator who is known for pushing people to believe in their inherent power to lead a purpose-driven life. She has written several articles for the Jamaica Gleaner and has received numerous writing awards including, the Lay Magistrates Essay Award. She is currently working on her first book, *This is My Now,* which will be published in November 2017.

Most of her early life was spent in less fortunate circumstances which led her to develop a burning desire to help people realize their greatness. She fervently believes that it is not where you start that determines where you finish, but how much you desire to leave the starting blocks.

The Seed
By Brooks Gibbs

*Winter recognized his purpose and time in this cycle
of life were quickly coming to their end. Spring, the
season of new hope and rebirth, was rapidly
transitioning into its full glory. The slumber of the
short and cold winter days began to awaken as the
warmth of the sun extended its daily visit to the
garden. In the garden, the apple tree had patiently
rested in her peaceful slumber through the winter's
respite. Now fully rested the tree, with great
excitement and anticipation, went to work becoming
the master of her purpose and creation, to propagate
and expand, to bring forth the fruit of her labor that
hosted the universal and eternal power of
creation...**The Seed**!*

I discovered the power of The Seed and the incredible lesson it holds
by traveling through a very deep, dark and difficult journey in my
life's experience; **The Journey Through The Dark Night of the
Soul**. At times this journey placed me in such a low emotional state
of being that it seemed I could see and feel no light. I wanted NOT
to exist, physically or spiritually.

Understanding the power of The Seed is knowing your personal
purpose, spiritual encoding, and choosing into being this. I know
each of us in this life's experience will at some level come to walk
through the Dark Night of the Soul. There is a time when we each
will question our value, our worth, and the purpose of our existence.
Far too many individuals struggle to find the answers to these
questions, eventually lashing out in anger and pain. Through these
moments of lashing out our world experiences violence, bullying,
domination, manipulation, control, loss of hope and yes, loss of life.

The Seed is a story I share in comparison to the journey of the apple
tree and her seed. All things follow a natural order and when we
flow with this natural order, peace and joy also flow in harmony
with our experience.

The snow, now melting and transforming into the life sustaining fluid, water, treks its way back into the blanket of soil that held onto the apple tree's roots. Her thirst now quenched, the apple tree could focus on the mission...bear fruit! She would hold the seed and protect it long enough that it could mature and fulfill its purpose to become the next apple tree.

The branches of the tree brandished their buds that burst into the blossoms of life, inviting the bees to come and partake of the flower's nectar, and in the process pollinate the tree, beginning the gestation of the Seed.

Like the experience of the apple tree in the garden, our experience of life begins in the spring. As a young soul, we experience life through the protection of the fruit of our family, friends, and neighbors. This protects most individuals from the challenges of the world and provides a space to learn, be nurtured, be taught, and to mature to a place where we begin our transformation and take on the opportunity and opposition in life.

The Seed spent its spring and summer surrounded by the protection and sweet goodness from the fruit of the apple. Protected from the gusting winds, rain from the storm, excessive heat from the sun, the deep chill of a cold night, and the hunger of a bird seeking its next meal, the seed grew and matured preparing for its time to transition, transform, and become the fullness of its purpose: to stretch forth to be an apple tree and continue in its contribution to this amazing world and the cycles of life.

Life for me as a child and young adult was a magnificent experience of exploration and learning. I was raised in the small town of Kaysville, Utah. On Main Street was a drug store that had a soda and malt counter, penny candies, and small toys. As a child, I found myself spending what little money I made from odd jobs on treats and trinkets.

Kaysville was seated at base of mountain, so there was always somewhere and something to explore. Forts and tree houses were built, pollywogs caught and left in a glass jar to see them turn in to small frogs, before letting them go back in the pond where they were originally discovered. Every field was a new territory, each hollow was new land to explore, every pond was a place to fish and make a rope swing.

I grew to young adulthood and found great times with friends in high school, at dances, basketball and football games, making spook allies, water slides, and many other activities that entertained and created great fun. Yes, life in my protective bubble was perfect!

Excited at graduation from High School, I was ready for the same excitement in my future. For a while it was great fun and there was new freedom to be experienced. I settled down with that special person, creating our own home, family, and memories. I moved through the spring and summer of my life experience.

> *Summer passed. The apple matured and now the sun was spending much less time in the garden. The exhausting work of the apple tree in propagating, protecting, and preparing the Seed for its destiny was quickly coming to its end. Fall was now the time of letting go! With a mix of sadness and hope, the tree released each apple from her loving care to begin the transformation of the Seed.*

> *At first the Seed did not recognize the change. Yes, it had felt the sudden jolt from the impact of falling to the ground, yet this had no immediate change on its environment. However it wasn't long before the environment quickly began to change. The fruit of the apple that had provided the protection quickly rotted away, and the Seed became exposed to the real world, with its contrasts of opportunity and opposition. The Seed felt naked and alone. It held to the memory of what once had been. The tree, once the protector and provider released her leaves, which fell to the earth*

and covered the Seed, becoming the blanket of fertile
soil that would hold and nurture the Seed in its new
*experience. In this dark and damp place **the Seed***
now felt buried!

What I found was with each New Year and each new milestone of life as a family, there came more pressure to perform, to provide, and to protect. Being young, intelligent, and strong I kept up with the new challenges as they came. I continued to grow and provide, however I was losing my identity as I kept trying to survive the constant strain of life and its challenges.

My personal value diminished rapidly and I felt more and more like a slave to everyone else, providing for their happiness at the expense of my own. These created feelings of anger and resentment that crept into my daily life. I began to feel that I must be unworthy and sinful. God would not let this happen to someone who was living correctly, therefore I must be a bad person. This opened my mind to those voices that often screamed inside of my head, "Brooks, you're not enough and you never will be enough!" Every little thing I did, I allowed the negative voice to criticize me and bring me down.

I pleaded with God to help me get rid of the voice and negative feelings; all along I expected God to take care of this for me. In a four-year period, I lost my mother, my father, and older sister. In 2008, the economy went into a recession and my brother and I lost a business that we had built over 10 years, forcing me into personal bankruptcy. I chose the role of a victim, so my attitude and anger led to a divorce and separation from my family and friends of over 25 years. I was single, un-employed, and homeless, living in a small bedroom at my sister's house, unable to pay rent or any other form of compensation. Drugs were not an option for me, so sleep and food were the greatest relief from the emotional pain. To awaken in the morning and face a new day of excruciating emotional pain was unbearable. At this point in my life I truly wanted to cease to exist. My pleading with God had changed from, "Please get rid of the voice to …. Please get rid of me!" I felt dead, encased in a coffin and buried by life!

The Seed lay there in the ground in its own self-pity

*and despair, waiting for someone or something to come and save it, to dig it out, and unbury it. Its desire was to relinquish its control and freedom to grow in exchange for the feeling of being protected and safe. Where exactly the thought came from is not known, however the seed began to recognize its power and its potential did not reside in the circumstance of the moment, but rather in the perception it held to and the choice made in each moment. The Seed recognized "I am NOT buried.....**I have been Planted**! I am not a Seed, no, I am an Apple Tree!" In this moment of recognition, the Seed redirected her thoughts from being a victim of opposition to becoming the victor of opportunity! Focused on who she was, an apple tree, the greatest apple tree, The Seed called out to the universe,*

"I AM AN APPLE TREE, DESTINED TO BE THE GREATEST APPLE TREE IN CREATION. WILL YOU BRING TO ME ALL THAT IS NEEDED FOR ME TO CHOOSE INTO AND ACT UPON, TO STRETCH AND GROW, TO BECOME THE FULLNESS OF MY PURPOSE!"

With new vision, the Seed now recognized the moisture was there to soften her husk allowing it to break free from her limiting beliefs and shell of fears. The soil that felt heavy on her shoulders was there to sink roots deep to hold her firm and solid as she reached and stretched for the light that she knew was there just beyond her current vision. From the nutrients and gift of the fertile soil she reached towards this light. As she grew and stretched for the light, the earth retreated, providing a path to this light and love that would provide the sustaining energy for the Seed to grow to her fullest potential.

Now as the tree emerged through her choice and actions she matured and became a part of the orchard of life. Joy is the gift of wisdom that came from the experience of the Seed.

What brought me out of my deep depression was realizing that if I wanted to change my life, my circumstance, I had to change my thinking. I had to let go of the blame and victimization that I was in, holding to my memories of the security of my past, in order to find purpose in my life of the present and future. It was up to me to see the divine and powerful person I was, deep inside. My circumstances do not dictate my self-worth; rather, my heart, mind, and faith, coupled with my new choice and action create my joy. If I hold onto my truth and declare it to myself and others, I soon found myself moving towards those things I declared. What I declared, I had to know! I choose to know who I truly am and where I want to go. In essence, I found my **Seed of Truth**, my declaration, my state of being. It guides me in all things, decisions, thoughts, actions, and relationships.

> **"I am a powerful, passionate, kind, and loving man. My purpose is to create a world of harmony, peace, and love. Through sharing the passionate and loving man that I am, others will come to know and feel their divine light and nature. Together we will share our light, and together we will create the experience of harmony, love, peace, and joy. "**

My life is now filled with greater joy as I strive to **BE** my purpose. My decisions are much clearer to make, and I measure them against my compass, my Seed of Truth, to insure I continue to move toward my desired destiny. I no longer feel hidden behind the false façade of measuring my personal value in people, places, or possessions. I know who I am! I strive to live this in every moment, every thought, every conversation, and every action.

You can know your Seed of Truth. You can know your purpose and power. As you do, you will create the experience of joy in the journey. Life is a great gift once you discover and hold on to the truth of who you are! I pray you may take on this challenge and find the joy of the journey.

Brooks Gibbs is an international presenter, motivational speaker, personal and business mentor, and international author. More importantly he is a Lover of Life, Learning, and People.

Brooks sees the world we live in as our teacher. Simple examples in nature and life-experience teach great lessons that, when taken in, bring Harmony, Peace, and Joy to your experience. These lessons open your heart to know that there is always a path to follow; there is always an answer to be received; and there is always a friend and mentor to love and support you through the many transitions and challenges of life. He brings these Little Lessons of Life to you in simple and effective stories that teach principals of how to make the journey of life an experience of joy.

Brooks believes in "digging in" and working with you to turn challenges into triumphs. Through his "Gentle Soul and Healing Heart," he helps individuals to open their minds and thought processes, by asking the right questions and encouraging them to find their own unique answers to the challenges they face.

Brooks will help you realize that the road blocks and walls of life are first solved by opening up your thoughts to new possibilities and stepping into trust. He will help you realize that you can move through the challenges with a new direction that comes from within yourself. Contact Brooks and begin the journey of positive change in your path.

As a Life Coach, Brooks shares this message and the process whereby he discovered his Seed of Truth. Discover your Seed of Truth by visiting this link:
  https://little-lessons-of-life.thinkific.com/courses/the-seed.
Use the coupon code "discover" and receive this course for free.

Email Brooks at: www.brooks.gibbs@littlelessonsoflife.com

You Are Meant for So Much More!
By Maxine Nwaneri

I couldn't believe what I'd just heard…

I was in shock, looking into the bulging eyes of this man, who had casually laid out the most horrific career options to me and my friend…

I was homeless, struggling with addictions, broke, and at such a low point in my life, that though his suggestion of achieving "financial freedom" through prostitution while working for him shocked me to the core, I struggled to see any other options given my circumstances. As I stood there, terrified, paralyzed, and feeling totally helpless to my crushing circumstances, I heard a voice within me say:

"This is not who you are meant to be! You are meant for so much more!"

In that moment, without really knowing what I was going to do, I turned and walked out of that room. And I have never looked back…

"You are meant for so much more!"

The still small voice of God had whispered that to me my whole life, but until that moment nearly 20 years ago, I'd never really listened, never really acted on it. The circumstances always seemed too tough to overcome. Instead of trusting the voice within, I subconsciously looked out, and let situations, people, books, school, magazines, TV, movies, and all sorts of external influences, dictate who I could be, what I could have, the kind of life and future possible for me.

I lost all sense of who I really was, and what I was even meant to be doing in the world.

All I knew to do was react to the circumstances life presented me, and effectively be led by them. And so they led me from one sorry situation to the next, until that night, when they led me to that dark room in London. There my circumstances suggested that my next step was to crash further into rock bottom by working for this pimp.

It was time to come to my senses! So when I heard, "You are meant for so much more!" I decided enough is enough!

I'm ready to trust...
I'm ready to listen...
I'm ready to see where this leads...
In that moment of decision I discovered the powerful overcomer within me.

Guided by this inner overcomer, God, and many incredible coaches and mentors along the way, I went:

- From dropout to straight-A student, and eventually a graduate of one of the most prestigious universities in the world, Cambridge;
- From being bound by all sorts of addictions to being set totally free;
- From seemingly no real career options to a successful International Corporate career;
- From having few real friends to being blessed with thousands of friends from all over the world;
- From not able to hold down a relationship to marrying the man of my dreams while hundreds of our friends from 55 nations looked on;
- From a total mess to having way too many blessings to list here.

One thing I realized on this journey of overcoming hopeless situations to finding tremendous success is that,

ANYTHING we truly desire is possible and available for us.

Although, with almost everything I have been blessed to achieve, I found that before the breakthrough, there are almost always circumstances that suggest it will be impossible. It's been necessary to mix desire with faith, and to trust God's leading and His voice which still tells me,

"You are meant for so much more!"

That voice, that message, is why I started my business, and what keeps me going when times get tough today.

In the second half of 2015, after having my beautiful daughter, I went from a high-flying corporate career to becoming an exhausted, intellectual-conversation-starved, stay-at-home mum who constantly wore mismatched work-out clothes, with no intention of working out. Some days I barely recognized myself in the mirror.

I looked around for hope, at other women in groups on and offline, and noticed something that troubled me. Many women are grateful for the blessings they have, like I was for my precious child, however, way too many of them, myself included at that point, let their own dreams die -- no, in fact be killed by their circumstances. Popular "dream killers," like perceived lack of time, support, finances, or naysayers who stifle our dreams, led many of us women, with such incredible potential to settle for less than we could achieve in life.

I felt like I was in that dark London room again.

Led by my circumstances, once again, I was at the point where I lost all sense of who I really was, and what I was even meant to be doing in the world. But this time I had millions of women "confirming" that the need to sacrifice my dreams and potential for my family was the only way forward. I knew I desired so much more for myself. I heard loud and clear once more within me

"You are meant for so much more!"

As with all my other successes, I gave the overcomer within me permission to rise up, and I sought divine guidance, got coaching and mentoring, invested in my skills, and took action. Within a few months, my International Speaking, Training and Coaching Business, "The Future is Greater," was born.

Time and time again, I have seen the incredible impact of trusting that "knowing" within that I am meant for something great, and empowering the overcomer within me to rise up and make it happen. Over and over again.

It breaks my heart to see women all over the world effectively being victims to their circumstances because they don't realize there's another way. My mission for my business is to raise up a tribe of "Overcomers" who are no longer available to be led from one sorry situation to the next by their circumstances.

I am passionate about helping these Overcomers do two things:

> **1-** Decide that The Future is Greater, regardless of how things look right now, and
> **2-** Go ahead and make their desires happen by using my 7-Step GREATER Future System.

I developed this simple, yet powerful system I use when I am invited to speak internationally, and in my work coaching clients, following an analysis of my incredible successes and catastrophic failures over the last two decades. This analysis showed clearly that "success leaves footprints." I confirmed the effectiveness of my system through the study of successful people in every walk of life. These steps in my system are common to pretty much all those who succeed, and they work!

I use this system to help my tribe of Overcomers:
- Know with certainty that the voice within you saying, "You are meant for so much more," is right!
- Know the future is so much greater than anything you may be facing right now.
- Know you can figure out how to make what seems "impossible," possible.
- Get clear on your desires, and make them happen.
- Quit wishing, wanting, and watching others who are truly living, making excuses for why it's easier for others and not you.
- Know there's nothing you see anyone else with that's not possible for you.

- Know you are meant to live and love an abundant life.
- Know that believing is seeing, so you can choose to believe your truth which is, the Future is much greater than you can ask, think, or even imagine right now!
- Smile at the future knowing you and your family are prepared.

So far, I have been blessed to work with amazing Overcomers from five continents and my dream is to reach women across the entire globe with this message of hope, inviting them to rise above whatever circumstances may be holding them back to live out their best possible life.

For many of my incredible Overcomers this dream looks like:
- Demolishing fear and self-doubt to start businesses, ventures, and projects they have been meaning to for years, even over a decade!
- Figuring out how to balance progressing with their careers while starting a family.
- Getting what they want in and out of the work place by increasing their business and relationship skills.
- Making more money in a business that was previously draining their energy and passion.
- Creating the kind of impact they are meant to make in the world through their work, while living an incredible personal life outside of it.

If that homeless girl, who stood in that dark room could go on to achieve all I have, do the incredible work I am blessed to, and enjoy an abundant life traveling around the world with my family on a monthly basis, then you better believe that you can certainly live out your desires, whatever your situation is right now!

The Future is Greater once you decide it is!

"You too are meant for so much more!"

Believe it. Act like it. See it!

Maxine Nwaneri helps ambitious women demolish the obstacles in the way of achieving their goals, living out their dreams, and creating personal and professional lives they love. She does this using the same powerful strategies that helped her go from homeless, to becoming the Successful Cambridge-educated business woman, Certified Coach, and International Speaker she is today. She is also a regular contributor to the Huffpost on topics geared at empowering women to live out their best possible life.

Maxine is a dual citizen of Nigeria and the United Kingdom, but describes herself as a "Citizen of the World," having lived in several countries on four Continents, and travelled extensively all over the world.

She lives in Norway with her husband and Soul Mate Nnamdi, and their daughter Chiamaka.

Connect with Maxine using the below links:

Join her tribe of Overcomers in her Facebook Group for Ambitious Women "The Future is Greater" at http://bit.ly/TheFutureisGreater

Connect with her on Instagram: @maxine_nwaneri

Access her free video series: http://thefutureisgreater.com/videoseries/

Find out more at her Website: www.thefutureisgreater.com

Use Your Gifts to Change the World – One Moment at a Time
By Carri Adcock

The home phone was ringing but all I could do was freeze … please stop, please stop. Paralyzed, I just wanted the chaos to go away. I wanted the world to go away. It had become a scary place and I couldn't quite get a handle on how to navigate. I didn't know who to trust, and above all I'd lost trust in myself. This wasn't the woman I'd been before. And oh my, how did I get here?

I was afraid to live. I was afraid to move. And I was obsessed with figuring out and fixing the chaos. Why did my life on the outside look okay from a distance, while inside the house and even more, inside of me -- was falling apart? If only I could find a way to make it all okay. To make him happy, to get him to stop being so angry. I mean we were getting ready to have a baby, a family. But then we did have one, and it didn't change a thing.

I was living for others, and going spiritually bankrupt. How the heck did I get here? I couldn't see a way out and I certainly didn't want to keep going this way. I was a prisoner of my own mind. I kept up appearances; my life looked good. House on the water, pool overlooking the river, full-time-work-from-home lucrative high-tech job, nice cars, dinners out – all of the 'stuff' that showed success. And behind all this material success and pretty life, I was dying and I wanted out. I wanted to run. I now had a child, but I just needed a rest. I was able to juggle all the balls of career, home, etc., but with the addition of a child I just couldn't keep up appearances anymore. So I caved … and ended up hospitalized for a nervous breakdown.

What happened? This isn't how life is supposed to go. I was checking off all the boxes. Where was the manual? What was wrong with me? I saw all of the people around me and they seemed to know something I didn't. I compared their outside lives to my inside chaos and frankly, it made for even more insanity.

In my 'mind' at the time, my hospitalization was just a rest before getting out there again and trying harder to line up the life I thought I should have; life the way I thought it should look. I just needed a breather and I'd be out and at it again. I was certifiable at the time, so why wouldn't I believe that I'd be better next "go 'round?"

Definition of Insanity: Doing the same thing over and expecting different results.

Today, I can say it was by the grace of God that I ended up in that hospital. I could no longer do it myself, and it was the best thing that could've happened. What I know now is that I was missing something. Something bigger than me, something unlimited, something outside of my limited mind. And I call that Something God. I was trying to control everything -- my life, AND everyone around me...actually in reverse order. See if they were happy, THEN I could be happy. If they would just behave, well doggonit, I'd be okay.

What I learned over time with the help of mentors, faith, and a daily practice is that I AM okay. And here in the present I have the CHOICE to be the best me. I have the CHOICE to invite abundance in. I have the CHOICE to see and receive the gifts around me. My attitude is my OWN responsibility. And when I live from here, I LIVE.

I almost ended this precious life trying to do it all myself. I found myself in an extremely abusive relationship, in addiction, and in some very unsafe situations. And I volunteered for it. At the time, I'd say I was a Victim to it. And this 'victim' idea is what kept me marching my way toward death. When I played the victim I had someone else to blame, but the real deal was I had choices all along the way. And by God's Grace today, I know this.

When I finally let go of the reins, the wheel, the drive, the strive, the wishing, the pleading - things began to change. When I finally was open to the idea that God was in my corner, loving me and not punishing me, I began to see the truth in how blessed I am. When I finally let go of the outcome I 'thought' I needed in order to be okay, even better outcomes began to appear. I began walking with life instead of running from it. And the healing began.

I started a daily practice of writing a letter to God each morning, and share it with a mentor. I give Him all of my fear, anger, victim mentality, self-centeredness…whatever shows up. And He began to use it. These painful, scary, embarrassing events in my life that I wanted to hide became some of my greatest Assets. I've learned that my experiences are nothing to be ashamed of, and they can help others, so I share them freely. Early on this walk out of the dark, the first relief I received was the idea I'm not alone. I'm not unique, and this invited me back into the human race, and from there it has been such a beautiful journey.

When I was three-years old, I would stare at the small purple violets spread all over the wallpaper in our downstairs bathroom and imagine each as a person in a crowd before me. I told stories, I inspired, I laughed and waved my arms at the 'violet people,' and it was natural; my heart soared, and I felt at home in the action. I have not lost the desire to inspire, to share. Actually this desire resurfaced quite a few years back, unearthed in the process of being reintroduced to myself, the self that God put here with a purpose. And I smile each time that I remember that moment. I can return there – 42 years before, in a heartbeat.

I'm learning time and location are irrelevant in God's Kingdom. And I know that this sharing, storytelling, relating, is part of my purpose. I've been fortunate to speak in groups over the last few years. No planning, no outline writing, no THINKING. I've been taught to ask God for the words and show up, and so I do. As a child my audience was the wallpaper and now today those 'violet people' have been transformed into amazing people I've met all over the world.

Today, I am recently married to the love of my life, my best friend, and a man who treats me like a queen and himself like a king. I took a seven-year hiatus after my previous relationship to get to know me, and I learned how to bring me to a healthy relationship. Oh my, it was worth the wait! I was married in the redwood grove, 3000 miles from my current home; yet I had declared at nine years old, standing in that very grove, "If I ever get married, it will be here." Do not discount your own intention. God, the Universe, whatever you choose to call what is greater than you, is conspiring to bring it to you ALL THE TIME. I help people to clear away what blocks them from receiving.

I have a healthy 11-year old son who watches his mom live her dreams and mentor people along the way. He has learned to share his own experience as well – last year he was able to help a friend who was going to repeat a grade. He also went through that experience, so he found some time to speak with the friend and let him know he wasn't alone. He then proudly reported, "Mom, I had my first coaching session!" Our children always watch us, and what a gift to show them what is possible, to follow their heart, and that they are enough, they begin from enough. There is no catch up, there is only show up!

I recently (very recently) left the corporate world after 23 years and am diving into my passion. You see I was 'good' at what I did, but it didn't drive me. My inspiration is love and connection. My purpose is to bear witness to God's Grace. I work with people who want to live fully, to find their passion and go rock it out. I work with people in transition, those who are waking up to the idea there is more: more that they can contribute, more that lights them up. And they are READY to see what that is and go for it. This is not a dress rehearsal!

My life today is indescribable; it is unrecognizable from the woman who hid in the house, afraid of her own shadow, mind racing out of control, trying to figure it all out. I live today as the Roman philosopher Seneca proposes, "Begin at once to live, and count each separate day as a separate life."

And it began by believing it was possible; God doesn't give me anything without the tools to navigate it. Believing that my happiness is a choice, my attitude is my own responsibility and this has changed everything.

I work with people who want to live, who want to see this wonder in each day and the abundance that is theirs to have. I work with people in transition … building new businesses, new relationships, to get clear on their purpose and desire.

Success is not the zeros behind the bank account, the cars in the driveway, the homes in the locations, and the brands on our bodies. Success is the joy in our hearts; and with this joy comes the abundance that may manifest into all of the human measurements. Yet the material manifestations are just the bonus of a fully lived life.

I do not regret one experience I have had in this life. This doesn't mean I want to repeat some of them, yet they are the very experiences that allowed me to wake up and to live the life I am blessed with. When your heart leads you in this life your impact is immeasurable, and being ambushed by joy is a regular occurrence. Yes, life happens, but this too can be delicious if you choose to learn from the bumps, be curious, and gain more Assets along the way. I am a living miracle and my purpose is to shine a light on the miraculous in others.

Carri Adcock's personal story has shaped her life and given her gifts beyond her wildest dreams. She knows today some of life's most precious gifts do not come in a pretty wrapped package. Often the most precious gifts, most effective assets are the product of some of the most painful experiences. Inviting the gift in from these experiences, being curious about what to learn from them has transformed her story to one of adventure, fun, amazement, prosperity, and significant, present, meaningful, fulfilling relationships.

"My attitude is my responsibility and it has and continues to shape my life into more than I can imagine." Carri uses her experience and what she has been so blessed to learn to guide others to unearth and get to know themselves so they may be real, relate to the world, and make the impact they were designed to contribute."No one can relate to a facade". Carri has learned the richness of life by fostering relationship, which begins with her.

Carri is passionate about the life she's been given and her calling to guide others to a prosperous life of their desires and balance in every aspect of their lives. She continues to do the work in her own life so she may keep growing, and she is invested in showing up 100% to guide you in doing the same.

You can contact Carri questions@carriadcock.com
 or visit www.carriadcock.com

Receive your freebie here: http://www.carriadcock.com/freeoffer

My Self-Care Journey
By Dawn Palfi

Maybe being from a small town, you learn to appreciate the simple things in life. I was lucky enough to grow up one street away from Lake Erie. This was a place where I spent much of my free time. This too was a place that always gave me peace and safety. I visited daily, whether it was to be at the beach with friends, watching the sunset, or going for walks along the shore to search for seashells. Although, I didn't know it at the time, it was the groundwork for my self-care and self-love journey.

I do not recall the exact moment in time, but at some point my simple journaling of my thoughts, fears, and emotions turned into poetry. I had a passion for literature and creative writing. When I was younger, I carried a journal with me to a spot that overlooked the lake. There I would sit, in silence, listening to the crashing of the lake waves. Here, my thoughts, feelings, and worries would flow to paper. I wrote a lot about nature, heaven, and death. Yes, death. I was surrounded by it starting at a very young age. It was comforting for me to make heaven sound beautiful, peaceful, and alive.

Over the years, I began to see a constant theme in my life: people pleasing. My mother wanted me to have a better childhood experience than she had, so I was over-involved in many activities. When this was married with my perfectionist personality, it put me under a great deal of pressure. Activities were not fun, and I dreaded practices, performances, and functions. At one point, I rebelled. I always wanted to be a nurse, until I discovered that was my mother's dream as a child. So to cut off my nose to spite my face, I did everything in life but nursing. I continued to find solace in my writing and my visits to the lake.

As a child, I was always taught to do the right thing; don't hurt others intentionally and to never speak badly to anyone. Growing up with very strict parents, I feared stepping out of line because there were real consequences. Sadly, it cost me my own happiness and joy. Being a nice person meant, you always put others first, yourself last. So I neglected to take care of my own needs.

Love, was also a hard lesson to learn. Loving someone who is incapable of loving only sets you up for trouble. Empaths are usually the ones that feel they need to double time in these relationships. They show more and more love in order to receive the love back that their mate is unable to supply. I often picked the wrong men to love. I felt it was a challenge to try to compensate for the love they lacked. However, all I did was become miserable and resentful. I lost myself in these relationships. You cannot live in a loveless relationship and expect to feel content. During this time in my life, I began to gravitate, unknowingly, to the sport of running to literally escape my life.

For two solid years, I ran just like Forrest Gump. On the trails, my brain was distracted by nature, birds, hawks, and deer. This was my solitude. My brain could turn off, which was never possible during the day. Normally, my brain was flooded with thoughts on what was wrong with me to be in such empty relationships. When I ran, my endorphins were lifted, my mood felt lighter, and over time I was able to get through another week of disharmony.

I joined running groups, ran at night, during the day, in the snow, in the rain, and even in other countries. Racing was my new passion. Setting running goals made me feel in control when the rest of my life felt out of control. Crossing a finish line after months of training felt redemptive. It also helped me gain my confidence back. I was good enough. I was strong enough to finish. I felt myself slowly revealing the strong, independent woman I had always been. I started to regain my identity. It also helped me focus my energies on myself instead of someone else that was not even investing time in himself, let alone me.

So, my journey with self-love and self-care began. I read books, immersed myself in yoga, kickboxing, and meditation. I spent time at the lake again, just sitting in stillness, letting my worries wash out with each wave that rolled away from me. I unburdened specific issues that were weighing me down. It helped me feel lighter with each visit. I also began taking photos of the sunsets. I suddenly wrote my poetry again. I had stopped writing for years because I could not emotionally connect with myself. The pain was too deep and too difficult to face. When I could write, the words would flow through me. I had to quickly write them down so I would not forget. I had lost that ability for years due to my tumultuous relationship that I kept trying to fix. But during this time on my journey, emotions and feelings returned, and I had much to say.

Of course, your partner notices when you are working on your own stuff, and this can cause a lot of resistance. I was no longer the passive, fearful girl that was always waiting for a bone to be thrown her way. I made myself a priority since he made everyone else a priority except me. Turbulence and distance became the main themes of our relationship. Eventually, my races became a source of contention, and it was quite interesting to watch him try every angle to get me to stop running. I stopped informing him of my race schedule until a day before the race. The worse he tried to make me feel, the more I took care of myself. I was finding my way back to myself and he felt threatened. Running cleared my view and my path presented itself.

Around this time, a friend of mine introduced me to essential oils. I was immediately intrigued after hearing her story about how they helped both her and her son. I was actually looking for something to help my daughter with her inability to sleep. So, I became an essential oil distributor. I went to a seminar to learn more about the oils I would be using and selling. I was hooked and added a new self-care regimen to my toolbox. After months of reading, learning, and experimenting with my daughter, I began using them as well. Sleep was never so fabulous.

Once, on a training run, I thought about my writing. I had always wanted to share my writing on a level that would help people. I had a calling but was not sure what it was. I just knew that I wanted to help women like myself. And as luck would have it, my purpose was handed to me during a very odd time in the world. Prince, the entertainer, unexpectedly passed away. I was stunned. His music was an integral influence on my life and my writing. His passing made my search to find my life's purpose more urgent; another reminder that life is too short to wait for the right time.

Like many people, I planned to attend Prince's tribute celebration on October 2016, in Minneapolis. As I was on my flight, headphones with music firmly planted in my ears, I tried to figure out where my life was heading. So, in the midst of my flight, I begged God to help me. I asked Him to show me my life's purpose because I felt stagnant. I had a gift with my writing and I needed to share it with the world on some level. "But how," I wondered. I repeated this plea for several minutes. Lastly, I added. "God, no matter how difficult this change will be, I am ready." My life has been a whirlwind of changes ever since.

While in Minneapolis, I sat by Lake Ann and quietly repeated my plea to find my path. I felt open, free, and light. It was in Minneapolis where I met my life coach Dorothy-Inez. We discussed my many talents and my yearning to help women through my own life experiences and self-care passion. We immediately began to build ideas on how to make my dream of becoming an entrepreneur a reality. She not only coached me on my business but she also kept me on task with my own self-care routine.

By the time I returned home from Minneapolis, I felt different. I was happy, at peace, and rejuvenated. Of course, I was met with much anger from my partner. Within minutes of seeing him, he berated me on all my shortcomings as if I had done something terrible to him. I felt a fire within me rise up as he sat across from me pointing out all my flaws. I am sure I said a few choice words, but I was shocked at how quickly those words flew out of my mouth. Two weeks later, I received a text that I needed to find my own place to live. After 11 years with him, this was the way he chose to end our relationship. I was blown away.

I had sold my own house in September before I left for Minneapolis. But I started looking for a house of my own in October, and was moved by December. As devastating as this time was for me, I had literally begged for my path to be revealed, and here it was in all its painful glory. The ironic thing was that for the first time, I felt like I was really home. I felt rooted. I was free to begin working on my business and do what made me happy.

I seemed to work well under multiple ongoing stressors. Life will always deliver its fair share of stressors. It is how we handle them that makes or breaks us. And, those difficulties are always a fleeting moment in time; it is not a permanent situation. Life will get better if you are open to allowing it to unfold as it is supposed to, not how you want it to. That was a hard lesson for me to learn but one I will never forget.

Certain professions, such as nursing, require giving of yourself at work, only to come home and give more to your family. Being a nurse, I give more to others because that is what my job entails. But, I let it spill over into my private life as well. Some of us do not know how to say no. This was an issue that I worked on with my life coach. Saying no always felt bad to me, but also made me overwhelmed and resentful. If not careful, it can literally make your soul sick. Hence, "Wellness for the Soul" became the tag line on my business cards. If you are not well, neither will your soul be well. I consider myself a Soul Wellness Advocate/Coach.

The purpose of my business is to teach women the importance of self-love and self-care. I educate them on ways to accomplish both. I offer affordable products that will allow them to take pleasure in the simple things that often are overlooked due to the hustle and bustle of life. My signature essential oil blends can help them with relaxation or to feel more energized. My goal is to create signature blends for women unique to their own needs, such as dealing with anxiety, energy, and relaxation. I am currently launching a build-a-box concept, which includes items to promote self-care.

My wellness journey the last few years has been quite educational for me. I have learned that time does heal all wounds. When you continue to remain in unhealthy situations, your soul cannot flourish. Nor, will you be able share your life's purpose with others who may need it. We all have gifts to share; if you live a life that allows you to hide your gift, than what is the point of the gift? I strongly believe that there are no coincidences. Obstacles are placed before us to challenge us, not break us. Instead of asking why me, ask what is the lesson in this? What do I need to learn from this experience?

I am still beautiful despite the obstacles that were placed before me in a short amount of time. I chose butterflies to be a part of my logo to remind myself that being a strong woman means you can also be delicate without being weak. There is something freeing about self-love. If you can find love within yourself, you will never feel the need to be dependent on anyone else for that. It means that no matter what, you will always be happy. Practicing self-care and self-love is the best gift you can give yourself.

Dawn Palfi was born and raised in Ohio. She currently lives in Concord Township, Ohio with her three daughters Stephanie, Samantha, and Sydney along with their family dog Buster. She earned her Bachelor of Science in Nursing Degree and has been a nurse for more than 13 years. She created her business, Soulful Creations by Dawn in 2017.

Dawn is an advocate and mentor for women in educating them about self-care and self-love. In her free time, she is an avid runner and practices yoga daily along with meditation. She is currently completing her yoga certification so she can teach yoga as well as incorporate it in her business. She has a passion for essential oils and is an Essential Oil distributor.

Dawn is also an award-winning poet and enjoys photography. She loves traveling for both running races as well as for vacations. Often times, her travels are where her inspiration comes from for her photography and poetry.

You may contact and find out more about Dawn by email at: Soulfulcreationsbydawn@gmail.com
Or social media: Facebook@dawncreated, Soulfulcreationstore @Etsy, soulfulcreationsbydawn.tumblr.com

Misunderstood + Failure = Success
By Jane Richardson, PhD

I'm a quiet person, extremely private with introverted tendencies. I'm also an entrepreneur, expert witness, and author. Sounds contradicting, right? Well, it's true. And maybe this sounds like you as well. If you can relate to feeling misunderstood, drowning in failure, with just a dose of success, then my story is for you.

<u>The Launch</u>
With pure happiness and all the joys a fun-loving family could bring, I was a blessed to be the youngest and only girl with three older brothers. Honestly, what more could I ask for? The advantages of having three older brothers were enormous:
- I had protective bodyguards who always had my back and were ready to attack if needed.
- I knew the popular slang words and music before anyone else my age.
- I had the ability to tag along to events I had no business attending.
- I had social clout since older kids knew who I was.

<u>Misunderstood</u>
My three brothers and I were always together and it was the best childhood a girl could ask for. They were my heroes and I was their biggest fan, until the day I started to feel invisible. Slowly and painfully, my personality diminished and I began to disappear. The disadvantages of having three older brothers were noticeable:
- They were outspoken, charismatic, and able to capture everyone's attention … I was not.
- They had extroverted tendencies and were successful at making friends … I was not.
- They expressed their thoughts and experiences confidently … I did not.
- They told great stories with ease and made everyone laugh … I did not.
- They had recognition for accomplishing things first … I did not.

Suddenly the realization hit me like an avalanche. Could being the youngest and only girl with three older brothers be more of a disadvantage than an advantage? Did the perpetual spotlight shining on them cause me to accept a lesser role? Could this actually be possible? Known as the little sister, I was labeled, eclipsed, and misunderstood.

Eventually I disconnected from others. As my mother recalled, I stopped talking, kept to myself, and avoided socializing for months. Feeling comfortable by myself and enjoying the silence and stillness, time passed until the moment a significant discovery was made. I discovered none of the disadvantages was my brothers' fault. Repeat: None of this was my brothers' fault. Instead, it was my entire fault, 100% my fault because I failed.
- I failed because I accepted the role of being misunderstood.
- I failed because I was afraid to stand up for myself.
- I failed because I chose to live in their shadow.
- I failed because I struggled to be heard.
- I failed because I gave away my power.

Failure

I spent so much time thinking about what was wrong with me and why I felt like a failure. Days, months, and years passed before an answer arrived. Cue the drum roll, and hello reality check. The awareness that I needed to drop the childhood drama and become my own person was finally real to me. Forget the little sister label, I needed to transform myself and do it quickly. My sense of determination was urgent, yet a question remained: How does one become their own person?

At this point, I was a frustrated college student pursuing a business major that I did not relate to. As I prepared to withdraw from college, I felt hopeless and desperate. I thought it was time to abandon my dream of a degree and admit failure, once again. While preparing to drop out, I noticed a Career Magazine on the table. I read an article, written by Maria Shriver, who referenced communication as a career. This article became a turning point in my life as well as the inspiration to change my major. No longer did I need to drop out of college or feel like a failure.

Instead, I chose to study communication and immediately fell in love with the topic. Who knew classes like Effective Communication, Interpersonal Communication, Nonverbal Communications, and Persuasion could inspire such an intense transformation? This topic was a wake-up call because it taught me:

- How to use smart solutions for effective communication … to minimize misunderstanding.
- How to make an unforgettably elegant first impression … to capture the perpetual spotlight.
- How to communicate with charisma and sophistication … to be powerful and be heard.
- How to convey graceful confidence … to be my own person.
- How to be utterly unshakable … to create success.

Success

Not a single regret exists for the years of feeling like a failure because the struggles were worth the education. Learning **how to effectively communicate, stand up for myself, be powerful, and be heard were priceless lessons.**

We've all heard the expression "Communication is Key." Although this expression may lack authenticity, these three words transformed my life. An education in communication was my key to personal and professional success.

Personal

Sadness, disappointment, and hurt feelings exist in every relationship, but so do happiness, laughter, and good old shenanigans. Family, friends, and teammates represent the most meaningful relationships in our lives. Imagine how great it feels knowing how to communicate with them. A kind smile, pleasant eye contact, and solid listening skills may seem so obvious and magically effective. Just making others feel appreciated, supported, and genuinely understood keeps relationships strong.

Professional

Why I do what I do? Because my education became my area of expertise. With undergraduate, masters, and doctoral degrees in communication, I'm proud of my education and I have a strong understanding of the communication process. Three degrees later, I know effective communication is the number one, most important skill for success. It provides the ultimate competitive edge with clients and colleagues.

Communication
The ability to effectively communicate applies to every relationship and all industries including your family, friends, teammates, clients, and colleagues. What took me decades to learn is what I want to share with you. Consider it a shortcut to success. Here are my Top Three Keys for effective communication. The first and most important tip begins with you.

Tip #1: Choose to make yourself a priority
Talk to yourself like you would to someone you love ~ Brene Brown

- Relax
- Breathe
- Let go of fear
- Keep your power
- Let go of nervousness
- Believe you will succeed
- Know you are the very best
- Remove any perception of perfection

Tip #2 Confidence
It is confidence in our bodies, minds, and spirits that allows us to keep looking for new adventures. ~ Oprah

- Trust yourself
- Stop comparing
- Do what you love
- Know what you want
- Embrace your abilities
- Feel empowered by your skills
- Attitude is everything, so be awesome
- Be courageous and unapologetically you

Tip #3: Communication
The process by which one person stimulates meaning in the mind of another through verbal and nonverbal messages. ~ Dr. James C. McCroskey

- Speak with clarity
- Speak slowly and confidently
- Seek to maximize comprehension
- Seek to minimize misunderstanding
- Recognize and release signs of stress
- Channel apprehension into excitement
- Ask questions and seek honest feedback
- Review what you want others to understand

The Landing
Perhaps you're wondering why I wanted to share my story. Primarily, it's because I believe that my story is so relatable. Lots of people feel misunderstood and fail over and over again. My struggles are your struggles and your challenges are my challenges. We go through the same things. We have similar experiences. We are not alone. I was stuck in a challenging spot for years, and it was awful, but it also shaped me to become a better person. Once I dropped the childhood drama and picked up the courage to become my own person, BAM! My life changed, failure stopped, relationships improved, confidence peaked, personal and professional success arrived.

Every day, I'm grateful for the confidence it took to become a communication consultant/entrepreneur. And, if I can do it, so can you. It's a bond we share. Since my problem became my passion and my struggle became my success, I know the same is possible for you. Also, I know it's time to take control of your dream, become an entrepreneur and I'm here to cheer you on. As a sign of encouragement, I want to share with you my Four Keys to entrepreneurial success. Once again, the first and most important key begins with you:

1. Turn a struggle into a skill.
2. Pursue a passion.

3. Develop an area of expertise.
4. Enjoy success

Don't waste another second. Go after your dream. Trust yourself.
Become an entrepreneur. Use your struggle to help others. Embrace
your passion. Share your expertise. Create a career you love. You'll
be surprised at your success.

PS: I believe in you and good luck!

Jane Richardson, PhD specializes in effective communication. She distinguishes between effective and ineffective communication and makes the complex message clear. In 2003, Jane founded Clearly Communicating, LLC which provides highly specialized communication solutions for entrepreneurs, private companies, government agencies, and legal communities.

With decades of experience working as a communication consultant, expert witness, Fortune 500 consultant, Capitol Hill professional, college teacher, and volunteer, she had the pleasure of collaborating with multiple organizations including: IBM, the U.S. Presidential Campaign, the U.S. House of Representatives, Bristol-Meyers Squibb, Ortho-McNeil Pharmaceuticals, St. Jude Children's Research Hospital, Arnold Palmer Spirit of Hope, and Industrial Sales and Manufacturing.

Educated in the U.S. and Europe, Jane Richardson, PhD has a strong understanding of the communication process including communication apprehension, public speaking, persuasion, message analysis and delivery, clarity and comprehension check, and verbal and visual coordination. If you what to know what message was really communicated, just ask Jane.

To learn more please visit: www.clearlycommunicating.com

Seeking Truth
By Jennifer Gardner

Have you ever dreamt you were flying?
That moment you lift up off the ground, feet dangling, feeling a bit off balance, with the sensation that you might topple over. The feeling of weightlessness and freedom as you see the ground falling away from you. The sensation of moving in whatever direction you please. The moment you realize flying is actually possible, that controlling your movements over land and through the clouds is everything you knew it would be. You hear the birds and distant sounds of civilization. Then abruptly you wake up feeling exhilarated. That dream was your unconscious telling you to trust. In that moment of flying, you were happy, you had clarity and you didn't care about what was to come. You were living in the moment, truly enjoying the blissful awareness and euphoria. How would you like to experience that feeling every day? Complete freedom from stress, worry, and responsibility. It's my dream to fly, in every way possible.

[Fear: the conflict between a desire and a limiting belief]

Three years ago, I could not imagine my life as anything different from what I had always known. I had unhealthy behaviors set around money, confidence, self-esteem, self love, and relationships. I had bad habits and poor judgment. I came from a background of struggle, lack, and multiple abuses (sorry mom). It's no one's fault, and I am grateful for who I am today because of it.

The proud birth of my daughter in 2014, prompted me to change my future's timeline; to do whatever it took to become a healthy and successful mom, wife, and business owner. I only had a matter of time to do the right things to fulfill my dreams. The problem was I didn't have any specific dreams. I wanted to be wealthy and travel. That was it. I had no clue how to accomplish it, or even how to just become a healthy individual. I sought out a Christian life coach (after 12 years of non-helpful therapy) and read all the self-help books I could.

I came to realize that I harbored and identified with beliefs about myself and my life that were lies. I built my self-worth around these faulty beliefs that formed from years of filling my head with the wrong thoughts, and training myself to ignore my intuition. My self-talk kept me in a negative state of being and saturated every cell in my body to consistently feel sorry for myself; to make excuses; to blame others; and to not take responsibility for my life. I had been on autopilot. And it was simply my thoughts. Now that sounds like a simple answer, but it's an incredible leap to make this conclusion.

As a child, I had the most detailed and memorable dreams. I would eagerly and excitedly try to share them with my mom, but I remember feeling like she didn't listen or have an interest, and that was hurtful. The feelings of being unheard, the stresses of my home life, the divorce of my parents at a young age, and being bullied in grade school, along with a multitude of similar experiences, crushed my confidence. I truly felt that I was not good enough and that I was not likable. That mindset spilled into every vulnerable space in my life and followed me around for more than 30 years, causing depression, sadness, guilt, anxiety, self-hatred, rage, anger, frustration, and toxic behaviors.

I was stuck. I didn't know what to do about it; no one had ever shown me how to combat all the things I hated about myself. The black hole was deep, and the struggle was the conflict between my true and healthy inner being and the wrong beliefs that were encoded in my brain. My anger, fear, and doubt ran rampant throughout my cells. It checked all my parts and relationships and thoughts. Every day was a struggle. All the past abuse and stress, the screaming and fighting, the mental, physical, and sexual abuse, the death of my alcoholic father, the extreme personalities that I grew up around, and the buildup of layers of negative experiences with negative emotions led to a hurting, miserable, sad, and lost little girl.

I always had my faith.

"For I know the plans I have for you," declares the LORD, "plans to prosper you and not to harm you, plans to give you hope and a future."
Jeremiah 29:11

Have you ever wondered what faith really is? Seeing without believing, right? Well, it's more than that. It's *choosing* to believe. It's trusting that our path is in alignment; even when we don't believe it is, that it's *still* in alignment. That's the main strength I've had my whole life: Faith. During college, I made a commitment to *choose* to believe in God, even when I didn't feel like believing in Him. That choice brought me out of my deepest and darkest moments, because when I wanted nothing more than to dwell on my pain, I could trust that I would make it back out again, and that someday I would share it with others.

Being stuck in life with hurt, sadness, and pain was a magnificent place to be! I was challenged to get unstuck; to find my flow; to find my truth; to find my intuition. I finally dug myself out with one simple tactic: Asking. I asked God, myself, and my unconscious mind how I could change. I also asked other powerful "what" and "how" questions, and soon recognized that putting those thoughts out there returned the energies that I was looking for. Matthew 7:7 in the Bible says, *"Ask and it will be given to you; seek and you will find; knock and the door will be opened to you."* The Law of Attraction would agree fully that we are extensions of God and creators of our reality. The Bible also says in Psalm 37:4, *"Take delight in the LORD, and He will give you the desires of your heart."* The Law of Attraction states that "you get what you focus on, so focus on what you want." By choosing the right words and thoughts, I am now able to stabilize my emotional state and become more present in the moment. And then I discovered neuroscience.

Changing the brain.

[Belief; a thought that has been repeated until it's believed]

With coaching, I first learned that I truly and fully did not love myself. After coming to this realization, I knew I had to find a pathway to do so. That path started with simple affirmations and changing the thoughts I had about myself. At first, the idea of saying loving and kind words to myself just made me want to throw up. It was sickening to feel that connection between my core being and the hard, distant, outer shell I had grown to identify with, because I was not conditioned to feel that way. I needed a shift. So, I started looking for more answers, but answers to what? My purpose? My happiness? What reasons did I have to keep my faith or to pursue fulfillment? I didn't really know. Ironically, my answer to change was understanding the physical pathways in the brain called neurotransmitters that carry thoughts throughout our body.

At the time, I was unaware of the structure of the brain, the way God has laid it out. There are more neurotransmitters in our brain and body than there are stars in the universe or sand on the earth. Once I realized that I can physically create new pathways to run new programs for myself, just by thinking new and opposite thoughts, I became determined to alter the map of my entire brain. I started peeling off the layers of negative thought, with help from coaches, mentors, and with sheer determination. As I slowly started to climb out of the black hole, love myself, and become healthy, it got easier to see the other side of the tunnel. I started to believe my new thoughts. That's when I discovered I want to help others heal in a profound way, just as I have. I want to impact the mindset of others who are lost or stuck or struggling with limiting beliefs and negative emotions.

So many of us are held back by the mental programs we obtained when we were young. There are ways to change and become that person you know you are deep down. Here are a few tips I will share with you to find some answers for yourself:

1. Be kind to yourself.
This was a big one for me; listening to all the negative self-talk. I gave that voice the name Marcella, and spoke directly to her in times of conflict. I quickly tamed it and my kinder self was able to step out.
2. Create daily intention.
This gives your energy an outlet. It puts a plan in your brain as to how you will feel, think, and behave for the day. Intention gives your unconscious direction in order to take action.
3. Meditate.
It may sound cliché but sitting in silent focus quiets your mind and creates space for improvement. I didn't believe it worked for a long time. Now, more and more I realize how necessary it is to balance

out my emotions and to recall the calm.

4. Know that life is as easy as you make it.

We make things much harder and more complicated than we want to. Remember to trust your intuition and make life easy by taking the path of least resistance.

5. Feel good and get away from the things that don't feel good.

The Law of Attraction says that we activate any thought or word we use, so stop those negative patterns in their tracks by taking a nap or meditating. And focus on what you want!

6. We are eternally incomplete.

We strive so hard to gain the sense that we have achieved our outcome. We always tell ourselves that we will be happy when we complete our next goal, but that is a faulty thought. Our purpose can only be fulfilled by living in the moment and doing what we can right now to find happiness.

7. Expect abundance.

Those two words have powerful meaning in and of themselves, but when you put them together, and truly believe them, you will not be let down. Just don't give up.

Seeking is the first step.

When we awake in the morning from our dreams, we tend to either let them linger and dwell on how they make us feel, or we forget them all together. They are not much different than the dreams we hold in our lives. Both make us feel. They speak to us unconsciously and they point us in one direction or another, so we should trust what our unconscious is telling us.

In struggling throughout the years, I was right to trust my faith and intuition. Even though my understanding of faith has changed and evolved, it's been constant. To trust means having the drive to push forward and really know that not only will life be okay, but life is meant to be pursued and we are meant to thrive in abundance. God will give to us the very next answer that we seek, if only we ask and trust.

So just ask.

Jennifer Gardner is a Christian Life and Success Coach. She is certified in Neuro-Linguistic Programming, Hypnotherapy, TIME Techniques and EFT. She lives in Michigan with her husband Eric and 3-year old daughter, Wren. Her skill trade is graphic design and advertising. Her interests are the Law of Attraction, and learning about every modality she comes across. She very much enjoys feeling good. You can contact her at limegreengraphics@yahoo.com

A Technical Transformation:
From Machine Science to Human Science
By Fan Zhang

This is me during the day: sitting in front of computer most of the time, writing scripts, drawing schematic, or laying out circuit boards, talking to almost nobody. In the evening, however, I visit or video conference with clients for their beauty, health, and wellness needs, or coach my team to run their businesses. I'm an electronics designer with a Master's degree in Applied Science, and an entrepreneur running my home-based distribution business to promote anti-aging. I'm happy in both careers, but being an entrepreneur gives me great joy that I'm able to help others, whether it is in health or business.

I have been a technically-minded person since I was young. I enjoyed reading all kinds of encyclopedia-type books by the age of eight, and devoted all my spare time in junior high to photographing astronomical objects. My astronomy club friends and I stayed up many nights hand-adjusting an old, low-precision telescope to take long-exposure photos of astronomical objects like the Orion Nebula. We ran our own dark room and developed photos. We even attempted to fix cameras ourselves.

One of my most wonderful experiences was traveling one March to the most northern town of China at the border with Russia, and shooting photos of the Hale-Bopp Comet and the 1997 total solar eclipse. I took a designated train that carried all the astronomy hobbyists from around the entire country to Mo He, the only place in China where the total solar eclipse could be observed. The temperature was frigid: -30° Celsius in the morning, and -20° during the day. I used the brand new telescope that our club invested in prior to this event, which weighed nearly 50 lbs. The only company with me was my tutor in the club, an elderly lady in her 60s. We got up at 3am in the morning, and stayed out in the freezing weather for hours to catch pictures of the comet. On the day of the eclipse, I stayed out for a full day, no tent, no heat, no running around, in order to record the entire process of the eclipse with my camera. By the end of that day, I felt excruciating pain in my feet and fingers, and thought I might lose them; fortunately I didn't. That determination and sacrifice shows how passion drives us. We can do anything, and conquer any difficulty.

The year heading into university was a big year for me, as I needed to decide what to pursue for my future career. I was all about optics, astronomy, and photography at that time, but none of those seemed a good career path in the eyes of my parents. I had to compromise, and eventually chose electrical engineering. I was not satisfied with my university, so I came to Canada alone at 20 years old and finished my degree in Ottawa. I picked this field of study, not because I loved radio, electronics, or programming, but because it was supposed to provide a good job opportunity, and it was cool and rare for a girl to be in this field. I did eventually grow very interested in algorithms, artificial intelligence, and programming after 10 years into the job, but pure hardware engineering has never become my passion.

I stayed over ten years in a corporate job, had my two kids by 2014, and found my comfort zone. I was never too passionate about my job because it didn't allow me to advance beyond what I was originally hired for: electronic hardware engineering. The job was not too intense, and not too boring, so I just stagnated there, making no other progress in life, until two things happened that brought my entire vision to a whole new level.

The first happened when my daughter was three years-old. I decided that I couldn't let her forget our native language: Mandarin. It is quite challenging to keep a parents' mother tongue for the second generation while growing up in an English-speaking society. I searched for solutions, and one of my friends shared a read-aloud program on Chinese ancient literature, the *Analects of Confucius*. I had tried to read such ancient texts before but failed. These texts are full of wisdom but were written three thousand years ago, and I thought, "How can a child understand those?" But the theory is simple; children don't differentiate between what's hard or easy to understand. They just absorb them all, like a song. I decided to give it a go. We read the text out loud for 45 minutes every single day for an entire year! I would have never done this, had I not wanted to teach my daughter Mandarin, but the rewards were huge! My daughter was very shy, not willing to speak, but she grew more confident, speaking up in class, and making many new friends. For myself, just from simple repetition, I developed comprehension on many parts of the book, and started to realize the wisdom buried in these texts still applies in today's world.

From there I went on to read the Tao Te Ching and a bit of Huang Di Nei Jing (the "Yellow Emperor's Inner Classic," the oldest and most important medical literature of China). The wisdom in this literature was so enlightening, that I was submerged in joy, and felt passion renewed in my heart! I went on to take courses given by Traditional Chinese Medicine (TCM) practitioners and advocates, and was totally fascinated by the philosophy and approach TCM takes to treat and heal diseases and improve life quality. I even felt compelled to pursue a TCM master's education, but because my family needed my paycheck, all I could do was take a few internet courses.

The second wake-up call happened just at the end of 2015. My company down-sized due to a poor economy and new technology. Nearly 10% of the work-force and most of the contract workers were laid off. Those who were laid off, all in their 40s to 50s, with kids in high school or university, struggled to land their next jobs. I realized for myself, that I either needed to move to a more people-oriented type of work where knowledge hardly expires, or stay at the cutting edge technology in my field, investing all my spare time. As a mother of two children, I recognized that I did not have the spare time needed to keep up with all the fancy new technology, even if I enjoyed it.

About ten months after that lay-off event, a friend of mine invited me to a business opportunity. I was open-minded and went to check it out. Just as I expected, the business opportunity was in direct sales, and I've always believed the direct sales industry uses entrepreneurship opportunities as bait to get people to spend money. After the presentation, I was surprised to discover two things. First, many people on this team were PhDs, university professors and researchers in biomedical fields, medical doctors, investment bankers, and financial analysts. Second, the business model was simple, not much different than ordinary franchises, with commission-based on sales volume. Third, the company used genetic technology (AgeLOC) to explain how botanicals affect and heal human body on a genetic level.

To me, it seemed like a marriage of science and Traditional Chinese Medicine. Many doubt TCM because it explains all medical topics from an energy point of view and can't be scientifically proven. Although the AgeLOC technology doesn't explain all TCM theory, it has at least taken an big step forward. That was when I started to carefully look into this business.

As Robert Kiosaki said in his book, *The Business School for People Who Like Helping People,* network marketing is an excellent field for people to learn entrepreneurship. It's a business school that requires no pre-requisite, no degree, and very little money. What it requires is commitment. With a trustworthy company and good mentors, ordinary people can have a path to make changes in their lives. I have also seen the business men and women in this company, who not only succeed themselves, but influence others to do the same. It's a very different lifestyle than a corporate job.

In the fall of 2016, I learned that my uncle in China was diagnosed with stage-four lung cancer. The most effective way to treat cancer is early detection, but for most lung cancer patients, by the time the tumor can be confirmed by medical imaging, it is already too late. Traditional Chinese medicine, however, has a way to detect and intervene in health problems at very early stage, long before they progress into cancer, and treats the issues with acupuncture and herbs. Unfortunately most people don't realize they can seek help from a holistic healer, so they let the condition worsen until it is too late to intervene.

The knowledge in TCM is really not that hard to comprehend; its root lies in the rhythm of nature, and the human body's interaction with nature. Unlike modern medicine, the wisdom in TCM can be learned by anybody; the methods of meridian massage can be practiced at home. The knowledge buried in the ancient literacy of TCM is a treasure to the world. The barrier that prevents that knowledge from propagating is the language of this ancient knowledge, the means to communicate it, and the lack of advocates who can teach the basics in a simple way.

Modern technology like the internet and social media platforms provide us with the solution. The teaching and practice of this ancient TCM knowledge and techniques have never been easier to acquire. With my background in technology and my unique personal experience in learning and accessing this ancient TCM knowledge, I can contribute to this solution. My challenge is in communication skills, but that is something I can build through entrepreneurship. I have made it my life-long mission to study and deliver this knowledge to as many people as possible, to bring the force of good to people, and Nu Skin's technology, training, and business model will help me get there.

Eight months after joining, I realize that the true spirit of Nu Skin's business model reflects one of the principal attributes of an honorable man as described in the Analects of Confucian. "Now the man of perfect virtue, wishing to be established himself, seeks also to establish others; wishing to be enlarged himself, he seeks also to enlarge others."

Once again I am full of passion in my heart, ready to step up and conquer whatever difficulty that I encounter, just like I felt as a teen-ager in high-school astronomy club. As I embrace this new joy and direction in my life, I look at my children and can't help thinking, how precious a person's passion can be. One day, I will guide them to pursue their own dreams.

Fan Zhang was born in China and now lives in Ottawa, Canada, with her husband and two beautiful children.

Fan came to Canada alone at the age of 20 as an international student. She is passionate about technology and science, and finished her Bachelor's in Engineering Physics in 2004, and her Master's in Applied Science in 2015. She worked at a private firm in electronic research and development for over 10 years.

Fan has always been interested in and studies the ancient Chinese literature. She grew passionate about oriental philosophy and medicine which drove her to become an entrepreneur, so she can help people, one at a time, in health, wellness, and business. She is now an advocate for traditional Chinese medicine and naturopath for illness prevention and healing.

Fan is a business coach with Nu Skin Enterprises, helping home-based business owners to build a successful business via social media platforms.

To find out more about Fan and her enterprises you can reach her
By email at fantasticwithfan@gmail.com
On facebook @fzhang021
Or at https://fantasticwithfan.wordpress.com

The Shine Impact
By Kierra Jones

"You're doing great, but let's wait six months to a year to talk about your promotion!" Those were the words I replayed in my head from an earlier meeting with my management team. Looking in the mirror, I watched my tears fall. I felt powerless like the eight-year-old girl, waiting by the window for her dad to come like so many "no-shows" before.

I was 24 years old and had relocated with the company four times in four years to various parts of the country. I sacrificed many personal experiences all while managing accounts of up to five million dollars and receiving top performance reviews in both my official positions and the extra-curricular leadership and mentorship roles I was involved in. To top it off, the VP of my largest client had just sent an email on my impeccable performance up the ladder.

So, you could imagine how disappointed I was with my management team, but mostly importantly, in myself. Where had the go-getter, first-generation college student, create-new-paths-when-doors-close Kierra gone? When did I become so "corporate-comfy" that I lost my passion and drive, content with a career roadmap, written by someone I didn't know, telling me where my talent was "supposed" to take me?

In that moment of doubt and frustration, I didn't know what I would do, how I would do it, or if I even could, but I knew I had to try. There was no way I could allow someone else the power to dictate my life and success or be comfortable in an organization that didn't appreciate my talent. I promised myself that whatever I did needed to be something I was obsessed with; that was the level of passion I wanted in my life.

I started with one of my first loves – jewelry and accessories! Growing up as a chubby, four-eyed, black girl with low confidence and a negative body image, shopping was a nightmare. That was until I discovered accessories! When I realized how I could take the boring plus-size clothing and make it my own with accessories, my confidence grew.

As I grew older and entered my college years, my walk changed. I held my head higher. I felt beautiful. In a world that tells us our true beauty is defined on the outside, I finally felt like I belonged. But the true gift was learning that loving myself was a pre-requisite to this journey called life. Wearing my confidence inside-out adjusted how I felt about my place in this big world and changed the way I wanted to show up in it.

It became my personal mission to empower other women to do the same – to Show up, Stand out, and Shine in this big world! To never dull their shine for the comfort or expectations of others. To define their own paths, break through glass ceilings of limitations, and transform the inner conversations they have with and about themselves each and every day.

So, in 2014, I established my first business – an online accessory style brand dedicated to helping female entrepreneurs and professionals be chic, stylish, and successful. For the next year and a half, while continuing to work in my soul-crushing, creativity-killing, nine-to-five job, my collection was presented in over 70 pop-up shops and I shipped hundreds of orders to customers throughout the US.

However, I still carried an empty space in my heart for the deeper work I just knew I was meant to do.

My work needed to be more than helping women shine through their style. I wanted to help women, who like me, had careers with organizations who didn't appreciate their gifts, talents, natural abilities, expertise, passions, and amazing, unique characteristics – their real shine. For so long in my corporate career, even with my success, I walked through the offices of many prosperous businesses wondering why I was there. What did I really have to offer? Why did they hire me? Was I really as good as my last performance review said? Did I really have the skill set to move up in the company? I doubted myself, my gifts, and my accomplishments every day.

Then, when I found my place online and started sharing my story with other women entrepreneurs, in both private conversations and group settings, I finally started to see my gifts come to life. My heart didn't feel empty anymore. I suddenly felt as if sharing my story and helping others to find and monetize theirs was exactly what I was meant to be doing all along. Empowering women came so naturally to me; when I spoke to them, the words of inspiration and strategy to help them succeed in a meaningful way rolled from my heart and off my tongue. And the feedback from women I connected with every day gave me a high I had never felt.

Yet, I still held myself back. For about four months I dreamed of transitioning into coaching and finally leaving my corporate job. But we know how our inner Negative Nancy can be. Thank goodness for my support system I call my personal "Shine Board of Directors."

You know how a company has a Board of Directions? Well my love, you should have a personal one too. These are your advocates who empower you to shine and don't leave you second guessing yourself, questioning your gifts, or drained of the energy and inspiration you need in order to take action towards the things you want. I remember having hours of conversations with my support team who helped me build the courage to finally own my power, change my reality, and change my life.

I realized that I had spent my life living up to the expectations of what success looked like in the college-to-corporate mentality. I was also trying to break the expectations of what a poor, black, plus-sized girl "should" be able to do. In my mission to impress one person and prove the next wrong, I missed out on an amazing realization.

That was the moment I was *born*. I had a purpose and my true path was already laid out. Instead of focusing on my inner shine, I was only focused on external factors, therefore limiting myself from my true power. And it was time to break free.

In 2016, I made the decision to leave the corporate world and start on a mission to create the lifestyle I truly desired and deserved. I wanted freedom of creativity, financial gain, time, and most of all, I wanted to support people that my heart lights up to serve. I wanted strawberry mango margaritas on the beach during somebody else's winter and summer getaways beyond my few weeks of vacation from work. I never wanted to feel powerless in the mirror, staring at a stranger again. I never wanted anyone to have the power to dictate where my gifts could take me or determine their monetary value, when the truth is, those gifts are priceless.

Today, I empower empire-building, world-changing, female coaches and consultants to up-level the way they package, position, shine in, and monetize their expertise. I help them build the confidence, mindset, and soulful strategies they need to claim the clients, impact, and gain the freedom they dream about at night.

These amazing women are coaches, consultants, mentors, speakers, authors, and course creators ready to own their power and step into their Powerhouse Shine shoes, or stilettos. For years, they have held on to their gifts, talents, skills, and expertise, either under-using it themselves, allowing others to overuse it, or under-valuing it all together. And now, they are committed to impacting the world in their own meaningful way by packaging their expertise, passion, and purpose into programs, services, digital products, and live trainings and events without leaving any profits behind along the way. I empower you to #MonetizeYourShine.

So if you ask why I got started in coaching, it's because I never want another amazing, talented, intelligent, gifted, passionate, special, and unique woman such as myself to ever question her power like I did so many times before. I never want YOU to feel like the eight-year-old me wondering if you are worthy of being loved, or the 13-year-old me trying to cover up your beauty and silence your truth because deep down you're longing to be invisible. I never want you to be the 24-year-old me, questioning your worth and skill set as if you weren't good enough to be successful, with your value only associated with a big corporate name instead of the brand of who you are. Or better yet, I never want YOU, to look at my story, as if I had some magic sauce that you don't have within you to get started!

You, my love, have a special shine within you that no one can ever take away, unless YOU allow it. You have the power to change your life, to change lives around you, to leave an impact on this world that is bigger than you, and that lives beyond your days. You have the power to uncover, unlock, and unleash your shine. No one can ever shine like you. It is up to you to own it, to use it, to impact others, and most importantly, to impact and inspire yourself.

Because the truth is when you shine, you empower those around you to uncover their light so they can shine to empower those around them to do the same. And the movement continues. That, is The Shine Impact!

So, how are you going to unleash your shine to impact the world?

Kierra Jones, The Shine Strategist™ is an author, speaker, entrepreneur, and CEO of Kierra Jones International, an online coaching brand. Through her private coaching programs, digital products, and live trainings, Kierra empowers empire-building, world-changing female coaches and consultants to up-level how they package, position, shine in, and monetize their expertise, also known as their *Shine*.

In 2016, Kierra went full-time in her passion of helping women strategically monetize their gifts in a meaningful and soulful way that allows them to unapologetically infuse their passions and purpose, without sacrificing their profit, creating the life and impact they desire and deserve.

Prior to this, Kierra managed multiple five to seven figure accounts in corporate sales and consulting for a Fortune 500 company. She then built her own online accessory style brand featured in over 70 pop-up shops, shipping hundreds of orders nationwide.

Kierra's life's mission is to empower women and girls to uncover, unlock, and unleash their shine so they can package their expertise and monetize their shine online.

For the coaches, consultants, speakers, & online service providers ready to finally break free of the sales blues, stop playing small, and confidently take action, serve, & shine online to sell in the easiest way ever & feel good about it, grab your FREE Shine & Sell™ Worksheet at bit.ly/shineandsell

You can follow Kierra on Facebook or Instagram @KierraJonesInternational and join her private community at bit.ly/womenwhoshine
Grab your complimentary Monetize Your Shine Session at bit.ly/discoverkierra.

The Road to Being Special
By Alicia Ford

I have been on the road to being special for my whole life. I always wanted to be special. I craved it. As a bullied little girl who prayed to be invisible, I also craved to be so special everyone celebrated me instead of hurting me. I wanted for people to look at me and say, "That girl is special. She is talented. She has something going for her. She is going to change the world!" I spent a long time trying to please people and perfect my actions so that they would say those very words. I longed and dreamed of the day that someone would tell me I was special.

As an adult I waited and waited for 12 years for someone to give me permission to be special. All of my actions dictated this desire. The desire to be validated and accepted caused a lot of bad relationships, both romantic and platonic. In my mind, being special meant you could be successful. Being special meant you could be a leader, a CEO, or a millionaire. Being special meant you were different and gifted - so gifted that people could not deny your talents. What I didn't know then, but definitely know now, is that only I have the power to define what makes me special.

I have always been fascinated with entrepreneurship. Owning your own business, to me, meant you were strong, bold, and fearless. You played by your own rules. I put entrepreneurship on a very high pedestal, because I wanted to own something for myself. I watched my dad growing up; he always had a business going. He had both internet and brick and mortar businesses, so naturally, I wanted to have my own side hustle. My earliest memory of working for myself was charging my parents to iron and fold their clothes. In high school, I did brow shaping for my friends, and in college I did direct sales for a beauty brand. I was a natural. I had an intuitive concept of supply and demand. I kept products in my room and left booklets in all the all girls' dorms. However, everything changed when I left my small college town in San Marcos, Texas and moved back to Houston, Texas. The playing field was so big, I did not know how to compete.

Through the next few years, I joined and gave up on three different direct-sales companies. I just could not connect with what I offered. I still searched for the "thing" that was going to make me special. I still looked for permission to BE special. I still did not realize that no one person, company, or event could make me special.

In 2008, I thought I had finally found that special place at a major retail company in the United States. I believed this new company was where I could be special. I was promoted faster than I could ever imagine; five times in only six years! I received praise and was told that I had unique skills and talents. For six years I rode that wave. But then I was fired. I was suddenly let go from my job. At that very moment, I was so devastated and filled with dread. I hit one of the lowest moments in my life. I felt I had lost my validation to be "special." I went from making more than $45,000 a year to a part-time job that paid me less than a third of what I made before. This salary screamed NOT special to me.

So why was I let go? Because I dared to be an entrepreneur. I dared to take a chance at having something bigger than me. I dared to find an outlet to use my gifts and talent to serve at a higher capacity. I dared to use my life lessons and life pains to help others dealing with the same hand I had been dealt. I dared to be special on my own.

Before I was let go, I had explored sharing my story and life lessons, so I watched videos about helping others overcome what I already conquered. When I lost my job, I used that moment in time to fuel my quest for my own special niche in the world. I prayed, "God, this cannot be the rest of my life. There has to be more for me. I know I was created for greatness, but what is it?"

Soon after that prayer, the world of coaching opened to me. I was blown away! I had never heard of life coaching or business coaching, especially not through the internet. I was scared but fascinated at the same time. I consumed as much information as I could. I wanted to learn everything about starting a coaching business. During that first year, however, I quickly learned that the $600 a month I made at my part-time job was not enough to help me invest in my new business. I could not hire a coach or someone to help me with my website. I found ways to work around this as much as I could, to the point I called myself, the "Backdoor Queen." I actually prided myself on how much I accomplished without investing money at all. However, I was burning out and running myself into the ground trying to do everything myself, but not knowing exactly what I needed to do to run a business.

After one year of-struggling and living not-enough check to not-enough check, I still was not making any money in my new coaching business. I did session after session to no end. And I WAS MISERABLE! I was overwhelmed by all the webinars and free information that was out there. I felt NOTHING that I tried connected to me and MY business. Something had to change! I told myself I would no longer allow money to be the reason why I could not improve and grow my business. I didn't know where the money was going to come from, but I did not care!

I had a lot of obstacles in my way. I had so much self-baggage and fear. I beat myself up every day about the things I could not do and why I did not succeed like other coaches in my niche. But when you are a recovering chronic-depression survivor, with daily battles of social anxiety, deep roots in people-pleasing, and a fear of rejection, you process everything as though something must be wrong with YOU. You process your failures as if YOU are a failure.

Imagine a grown woman who on the inside still felt like she was an 11 year-old girl, bullied, picked on, embarrassed, and made fun of every single day. How could she find her special place in entrepreneurship? Needless to say, even though I overcame deeply rooted depression and suicidal thoughts, I was still on my road to being special.

My journey of entrepreneurship has had its ups and downs. I drank the "kool-aid" of other companies' missions and beliefs. The hardest yet most rewarding step I took, however, was to drink my own kool-aid. I finally quit hiding behind other people, stopped making excuses about why I could not achieve goals, and started finding ways to succeed. That was when I started to see where my special was. I focused on what my unique gifts were and showcased them daily. If I needed help, I asked. I did not let fear of investing stop me from getting whatever support I needed.

These are just a few things I told myself:

- It is not hard to share your truth and your story.
- It is not hard to record a video, live-stream, or write a post.
- Don't let fear make decisions for you instead of letting GOD help you.
- Ask God for courage and strength. The Bible says, "Seek the kingdom of God first in all you do and He will give you everything you need." (Matthew 6:33 NLT)
- You will NEVER have the money to invest in yourself as long as you continue to BELIEVE you do not.
- I don't care how much money you make or do not make, STOP using a lack of money as your excuse.
- Let God HELP you. ASK for what you want.

Reminding myself of these lessons every day, gave me the peace of mind and soul to get up and do what needed to be done to take care of myself, my family, and grow my business. I got the courage to leave the part-time job for a full-time job that paid me close to what I made before. With the new job, I was able to fund and invest in my business.

Walking down your road of being special is a path of self-discovery. You learn what fuels you. You learn who are, who you want to be, and how you want to serve in this world. You find gifts you did not even know were gifts. You battle fears, you shed tears, you get angry, and you get burned out. However, you learn what makes you laugh, and what makes you light up. You learn how you receive real joy, and you learn where your "special" comes from.

For me, I learned to trust God more. I learned to trust myself more. I learned to forgive past circumstances and people who hurt and wronged me. I learned to use my stories as my special weapons against self-doubt and fear.

I want to tell you that you are special. I want to encourage you to do this one thing. Position yourself as the expert because God needs you to be. He needs you to show the world just how special you really are. He needs you to share your truth on as many platforms and stages as possible. He needs you to grow your influence so you draw people closer to Him. He wants you to have book deals and endorsement deals, sold-out speaking tours, and TV spots. He needs to you to BE SPECIAL!

Alicia Ford is a Mindset Strategist and Client Attraction Mentor to online women, coaches, teachers, and consultants. She helps them shift their mindset, position themselves as the expert in their niche, and up-level their coaching content by aligning their divine messages so they attract their Dream Clients and increase their profits.

Alicia uses her own past life struggles with chronic depression, suicidal talks, perfectionism, people pleasing, fears of not being enough, fear of failure and making mistakes, and unwise money decisions to inspire and empower other women to just, "Be Your Own Image" through the power of entrepreneurship.

Alicia is an introvert who loves handbags, mascara, aviator sunglasses, and a Great Cup of Coffee. She loves reading romance novels, listening to self-help books, and journaling. She is also obsessed with watching makeup tutorials and office supplies. Journals, and Planners, and Pens! Oh my!

"Position Your Divine Messages, Attract Your Dream Clients and Impact The World"
www.facebook.com/aliciafordcoaching

Pain to Power
By Kanelli Scalcoyannis

During a business trip to New York I finished up seeing a client with my colleagues, when the owner of the company invited us for dinner to one of the most prestigious restaurants in the financial district. So he divided us up saying, 'Kanelli you come with me,' and my colleagues were assigned to other staff members for a ride.

As the parking attendant brought around the car, I went to the passenger side, but my client came to the passenger side as well. I thought, "What? Does he want me to drive? I mean really, I am going to drive in Manhattan?"

But of course my client, a gentleman, had come around to open the door for me.

Now growing up in a Greek family where women are trained from childhood to serve men, it might be expected that I would miss these gentlemanly gestures. But the real revelation to me was that I went directly to the assumption that I had to be driver, in charge and in control.

This was my first alarm bell that something wasn't right, that I was out of balance, especially my relationship between masculine and feminine or yin and yang. I felt that I always had to be in the driver's seat.

At that time I ran the expansion of an Italian Fashion brand into America and Latin America. I worked around the clock to accommodate the differences in time zones. I also tried to be there for my three-year-old twin girls, was the main breadwinner for my family in the middle of the worst financial crisis, and worked for rates far below my worth. I was juggling work, home, domestics, cooking, and taking my kids to and from activities. My hormones began to reflect this imbalance.

My life was a series of rushing from one thing to another. Between my responsibilities, obligations, and getting it all done, I lost touch with so many parts of me and my desires. There certainly was nothing 'sexy' about it.

In fact I often think about those times, that many new moms completely understand, that I like to call, the story of, *The Hand*. Yes, the story begins at the time you finally walk away from the kitchen, brush your teeth, and sink into bed thinking "Yes, finally this is MY TIME," at least until a baby wakes up. But as you stretch out your tired body, to your shock and dismay your husband's *Hand* lands directly on your thigh.

Holy shit, you've got to be kidding me! I mean, seriously? My job is not done? My day has not ended?

Nothing, I mean, like *Nothing*, is screaming sex at that moment. And I would think, "Did you wine me and dine me? Did I dress up or get out of the 'mommy role?' How do I go from kitchen sink to sex diva?" But then I would convince myself to just get it over and done with, my monthly sex obligation, missionary position and no more please. I have no energy to be on top - are you kidding me? Where had my healthy sex drive gone?

I struggled with PMDD (Premenstrual Dysphoria Disorder) after the birth of my twins. At first I thought I was going crazy. I think I fell into the trap that most women fall in, prioritizing my obligations over my pleasure and joy. My hormonal health forced me to make ME a priority again.

So my journey for balance began; I started researching everything to find healing from PMDD. I went to a naturopath, changed my diet, got a coach and joined a top coaching mentor program. I did a ton of inner work. I studied the law of attraction, wealth consciousness, functional medicine, inner child work, and energy work. I redid my wardrobe. I caught up on my life, all the parts I'd left behind to take care of responsibilities.

Not only did my health improve, but suddenly everything improved: my relationships, my diet, my health. I became an open-water winter swimmer and competed in races. My husband watched me turn from a crazy lady to someone that was thriving and laughing again all month long.

I stopped blaming my country, husband, the system, and started making lifestyle changes. I became fit and healthy, enjoying my kids, and loving my life. I attracted others to participate in the doing, and when I really studied the Art of Woman, my man started making more money in a week than he had made in months. As I embraced more of my feminine, my relationship with my husband sky rocketed. I became a better mom; I stepped into a life of ease, and I was no longer running from pillar to post.

As I healed, other women started approaching me to help them do the same. Not only had I found healing, but I had found my calling. I saw a similar profile of woman: the responsible 'mover and shaker,' the ones more comfortable in their 'masculine' -- analytical, super-intelligent, practical, addicted to doing it on her own, and overburdened by too much. They too started shining and blossoming with ease and grace by simply understanding the power of their femininity and realizing the power and privilege it is to be born a woman. Unfortunately a man's operating guide is only going to burn us out. Women operate and shine with freedom, time, intuition, beauty, community, spirituality, and sisterhood. If we are constantly living in a man's driven environment, this will only diminish our light.

I studied with some of the world's leaders in women's health and empowerment. I was dedicated to becoming a powerful coach and helping other women to reclaim their femininity and power.

As someone that had 20 years of professional business experience, I knew I could help professional women get their lives back. I work with them in a different way, so they are no longer slave drivers inundated by perfectionism and late hours, but choose work that fulfills them, that gives them more energy. It was magical, I was watching these women move out of the overwhelming place of 'trying to do it all,' to living from a place of desire, doing what turned them on. They traded their whiny complaints about life's struggles with celebrations for living out their dreams. They felt more alive, sexier, and their relationships improved as a result.

During an interview with Gia Allemand Foundation supporting PMDD sufferers, the interviewer asked me why it was so important to me to support these women. I told her that, what my journey taught me, is that you can go to the doctor, and give him your power, taking the pill, and numbing the pain. Or you can choose the path to heal, converting pain to power, and in that choice you will find your path, your calling, and have a thriving life. You can receive more than you ever imagined possible, and take everyone around you higher.

I believe we can have the life we want; we just need someone who has been through it to guide us, and show us the way. Creating a life you love takes courage and with some support we can all do it.

Kanelli Scalcoyannis is a multi-passionate, intuitive visionary. She worked for 20 years as an International Licensing expert, setting up brands all over the world for prestigious companies such as Warner Bros., Disney, United Media, Nickelodeon, Italian Fashion brands, and more.

She was not shy to reinvent herself as a performing jazz vocalist and more recently as a Success Coach, Author, and Speaker. Kanelli is the owner and founder Luscious Life, a company dedicated to helping professionally-driven women to live a thriving life with more ease and grace. To find out more visit: www.lusciouslifecoaching.com or email her at kanelli@lusciouslifecoaching.com

Join the private Facebook group: Luscious Life for Women https://www.facebook.com/groups/182041498866473/

Kanelli lives in Athens, Greece with her husband and two daughters. She enjoys travelling frequently, clean eating, cooking, Turkish baths, live music, dancing, and open-water swimming.

The Power of You
By Sanura X. Dean

I didn't know who I was. I didn't know my destiny or my purpose, or even if I mattered. I was adopted at three months, and though I had very loving and caring adoptive parents it seemed that not knowing my birth parents took a toll on my self-esteem and self-worth. I felt like I didn't belong to anyone. In a world of billions of people, can you imagine not having any DNA ties to someone that you could claim as your very own? Can you imagine the loneliness and the longing for a place to belong, a place to be accepted by people who were just like you?

I grew up not realizing that I had an identity to call my own. Various people came in and out of my life with their negative messages of, "You are not good enough," and "You will never be anything." I believed it. Adopting this mentality caused me to look for belonging, look for my identity, and look for love. I would do whatever got me the approval of people. I would do anything and everything to be celebrated, because in my mind if I was recognized as valuable, that would mean that I was loved. I remember in middle school, I would bounce from one group of friends to the next. If it was the "cool" girls, I would pretend that I had it all together so that I could appear "cool," even though at times I didn't appreciate how they treated people. I didn't have the guts to stand up to them because then they would not like me, and I would be forced back into the feeling that I didn't belong.

Further on in my journey I realized that I was living a life of brokenness, in every area of my life. I tolerated broken relationships where I allowed myself to be mistreated, allowing the lies, the cheating, the back stabbing, and poor treatment so that I could feel like I was loved. I internalized criticism and untruths that were spoken over me.

Somehow, through the negativity, I still managed to discover that I was good at encouraging, empowering, and influencing people so they could be the very best in their own lives, and it made me feel good. But every time I shared my revelation it was shot down, so I resolved to hide the very gift that God gave me to bless the world. I played small because I was so busy trying to be likeable instead of sharing my power, my gift, my authentic identity with the world. I later came into the realization that these gifts were given to me by my Heavenly Father, yet I was blinded by all the things I allowed myself to believe.

But then Jesus Christ stepped into my life and He gave me hope and a name. He came in and spoke to my need to be loved. He spoke to my feeling of not being enough. He spoke to my brokenness and lack of identity. He called me daughter of the Most-High King. He called me his beloved, the head and not the tail, above and not beneath. He called me blessed and not cursed, a royal priesthood. He told me that my worth was far above rubies. He showed me that there is power in my identity; that I am someone in Him because He created me in His image and likeness. I realized from that moment, that once I tap into the power of who I am, there is nothing that can stop me. I can accomplish the things that He made me to accomplish.

I realized my authentic identity was made up of my God-given gifts, talents, and skills. I was able walk in my power, to walk in my truth, and be comfortable being exactly who God called me to be. I began the journey into manifesting my destiny and my purpose. I learned that to tap into my authentic identity was to begin cultivating all that God has put on the inside of me. It is the power to operate at my peak state and receive everything that I have always wanted in my life, the abundance.

Now I know that I don't have to accept the sloppy seconds of what people call love. Now I don't have to sell myself short just to say that I have friends. Now I don't have to worry about not belonging, because low and behold, once I stepped into my authentic identity and released the authentic power given to me by God, the door to find my birth family was opened and I was welcomed with open arms. On March15th, 2017, I was led by God to do a DNA test. On April 29, I connected with my first cousin through the DNA test and had lunch with her and the little sister that I never knew I had. By May of that year I went to my maternal grandmother's house where I was greeted with love and tears of joy, and afforded the opportunity to listen to stories of my blood genealogy. The power of being connected to the abundance of God did not stop there. On July 12, 2017, there I was, sitting in a room with the woman who gave birth to me, sharing, laughing, and loving on one another. I'm telling you, the hug that I got from my mother was a thirty-eight-year-old answered prayer. All because I listened to God say, "Be who I made you to be," and I obeyed. Once I stepped into my authentic identity, my unique message was birthed. That message is that with God all things are possible if you believe and act.

Yes, tapping into your authentic identity is powerful. You don't have to be who people say you are. You don't have to be who they want you to be. You do not have to do the things that others want you to do so that you fit in with the crowd. If you want to be successful, you have got to know that you are special, that you are unique. You must know that even before you were formed in your mother's womb, God saw a need in the earth, and He made you to fulfill that need. He called it your destiny; He called it your purpose. It is a place and job just for you. No one else has your message to share. No one else has your passion and zeal to get the job done. Realize right now in this moment that you are enough. Realize that all you must do, all we must do, is tap into the power of who we are to find your authentic identity.

I didn't know who I was, but because of Jesus, today I do. I am Sanura. I am a tender, warm-hearted, woman of faith who is not afraid to love. I am an encourager, sent by God to empower, propel, and teach other women that they are indeed powerful. This is my authentic identity. I am here to let them know, that when they refuse to allow anything or anyone to define who they are or dictate what they are meant to do, they are free to really find the power of authenticity within themselves. My job is to show women that they are enough to accomplish all that God is calling them to accomplish. I was put on this earth to help every woman learn that she is comprised of many gifts, talents, skills, and abilities, and she has an authentic identity waiting to be unlocked.

I not only found my birth family and crushed the lie that I was alone in this world; now I know what I was put on this earth to do. But while it is important to know what your authentic identity is, it is more important what you do with it. I am taking action to fulfill my purpose and destiny.

As I found myself awakened to my truth, I awakened to the possibility that I could live a life full of the greatness that dwelled inside of me. At that point, there were some questions that I needed to answer. Would I continue settling to play it safe and allow my life circumstances to be the reason why I missed out on fulfilling my calling, purpose, dreams, goals, and aspirations? Was I going to follow the leading of my soul, tap into the power of who I am, and begin doing the things that burned in my heart so I could see them become a reality? Or would I rather live out a destiny that was not meant for me?

I now pose these questions to you.

Are you ready to consider the depths of your soul and tap into your unique authenticity to find that power that dwells within? Are you ready to say no to fear and the feelings of not being enough? Are you ready to stop giving yourself the excuse that there is too much going on in your life to show up, and say yes, to fulfilling your destiny? Are you willing to give up ever doing and living out those things that are burning in your heart to do?

You can do it. You can make the commitment today to owning your truth, operating in your authentic power, and living a life of passion. You don't have to let your fire be snuffed out by the noise of what people say or think. Now is your time to shine. Now is your time to say yes to you. Now is the time to let God get the glory out of your life. Now is the time to manifest your vision with confidence and power.

I am mastering who I am today. I recognize that I am enough. I understand that all the pain of not realizing my identity, not grasping the truth of my worth and value, not living in wholeness, not feeling like my life had great meaning, and not feeling loved, was all for a greater purpose. It was meant to bring out the greatness in me.

You are meant for greatness. You are meant to get your message out. Get up and begin to tap into the power of your authentic identity, and you will undoubtedly come to find your authentic power. And with that power, you will not only be able to change your circumstances, you will be able to have maximum impact on the world. You will become the game changer that you have always longed to be. You will leave a legacy of strength, courage, and resilience for your family. Say yes, to manifesting the vision in your life. Tap into your authentic identity, your power brand. Tap into the power of you!

Sanura X. Dean is an author, Empowerment Coach, and Motivational Speaker with a heart and passion to help women live victoriously on a daily basis. She is prayerful in her approach with each client, actively listening to each need, and taking her clients on a transformational journey where they will have an opportunity to tap into the power of their authentic identity. She helps them discover a fresh feeling of accomplishment, success, and freedom as they realize their own unique place of power in the four essential core areas of their lives: mental, spiritual, emotional, and physical.

Sanura's programs use a Christian-based methodology to help women let go of self-sabotage, self-doubt, and feelings of being held back. She teaches each client what it means to use the power of who you are to release your manifested dreams, visions, and aspirations.

Sanura is a co-author of *Notes to Younger Women*. She has over six years of experience speaking to groups to inspire and motivate people to be their personal best. She graduated from the School of International Ministry in 2011, and received her license to minister the gospel of Jesus Christ. In the past she worked as a certified makeup artist and uses her creativity and knowledge of beauty to encourage women in the art of self-love and appreciation.

Sanura is a mother of four beautiful children. She enjoys shopping and spending time with friends and family. She is truly a lover of people and prays daily for all to live in the spirit of excellence.

Email Sanura at sanuradean@gmail.com

Beauty from Pain
By Johanna Stock

Life has a funny way of teaching us things. Each one of us has countless numbers of defining moments throughout our years on this earth. Looking back on my life, I know, if I had not ever experienced these moments, I would have never been able to push to become the woman I am now.

As a teenager, I loved life. I was driven by academics and sports. I had plans to attend a University on a soccer scholarship, and was excited about everything the future had to offer. Then, I was injured, and my soccer career was over. As my love for life was structured around that, I became depressed and lost the passion to achieve any goals I had. Within a couple of years, I became pregnant and got married.

Seeing my newborn son gave me a new love for life, with new goals and a new commitment to myself, that I would be the best mother and wife anyone had ever seen, regardless of my age. And, I did this. Quickly thereafter, I realized that the situation I was in was not the best one. Yet, I was determined to push through it for my son and my family. After I was blessed with another beautiful baby boy, the situation started to worsen. I couldn't figure out why things were getting worse, when I was doing everything I could imagine to make it "okay." I found myself becoming fearful, yet constantly excusing and justifying actions and behavior, forcing myself into denial, and somehow even placing blame on myself. I just needed to be better, work harder, be prettier; then everything would be okay.

People ask how individuals can allow themselves to stay in an abusive relationship for so long, but when you are living in a constant hell, you go into survival mode. You go through each day just trying to keep your head above the water, trying not to drown in the emotions and feelings of failure and confusion. You become very good at covering things up and playing pretend when you are around others. Days, months, years go by, and you don't even realize just how broken you are.

Nobody knew of the hell I was living in. As a mother of four young children, my focus was only on making sure they were okay. I excused the negative behavior, because I didn't want to lose my family. All I had ever wanted was to give my children the most amazing lives, the lives they deserved, and that meant keeping my family together, right?

When the abusive behavior started funneling into my children, I knew I couldn't allow that to happen. It was one thing to deal with an abuser on my end, but I could not allow my children to be in that type of situation. I knew I had to break free, but how?

I began feeling completely hopeless. And the situation continued to worsen and spiral out of my control. I had lived half of my life under fear, manipulation, and control. I was emotionally numb. I didn't want to feel anymore, because it was just too painful. I lost every part of my self-worth, my self-image, and my belief that I was anyone. Yet, I knew I was a good person. I knew every day I was striving to be the best mother, best wife. I lived with the mindset that if did all of this, everything should be okay, right?

But, no. Everything was far from okay. I became so broken, I didn't even recognize myself internally, anymore. I became suicidal; I didn't want to feel the physical and emotional pain anymore, I just wanted to die. I had broken. Yet, in my heart, I knew I was someone who didn't break. I knew I had to get out of my situation, but how? I had never been on my own, I had four young children. I was completely dependent upon my life and marriage. But, I knew I couldn't stay.

I had tried everything I could to keep my marriage together; counseling, separation, until I finally came to the point of realization that nothing was helping. I was terrified to completely end the process, but I knew I'd had enough. I just couldn't do it any longer. There were so many mixed emotions, initially. I felt unhappy, because I didn't want my marriage to end, yet at the same time I began to feel liberated.

Although the living situation changed, a lot of the issues did not. For years, I slept with a large knife under my pillow, just to feel safer. I lived in the unknown of whether I would be approached by my ex, or not. I was followed, and could not even feel comfortable in my own work place. I felt like I had to constantly be looking over my shoulder. Yet, all this did was fuel me to become stronger.

Everyone comes to a turning point in their lives where they are faced with a decision, and that decision can have a huge impact on the overall outcome. Mine came shortly after I had broken free, and terminated my marriage. I was trying as hard as I could to deal with my new situation, yet the continuous physical and emotional strain began to wear on me. Day after day, night after night, running on only a few hours of sleep, I finally crumbled, and every emotion I had forced to keep in, seemed to suddenly come crashing down on me.

I was at home at the time, with my four beautiful children, and in hopes they wouldn't hear or see me that way, I hid in my bedroom closet. I finally had enough. I was completely depleted of physical and emotional strength. I fell to the floor and began sobbing, uncontrollably. I had never felt so broken. I had never felt so alone, so scared, so confused, so hurt, so angry, so hopeless. The emotions came flooding in like a typhoon, and I just couldn't do it anymore. I prayed my children wouldn't hear me. I prayed I could gain some sort of self-control, so I could just push through. But, I could only cry. I had nothing left internally.

I started thinking about my beautiful children. I prayed that somehow, some way, I could be the mother they needed me to be. I could barely utter any words, but I finally spoke, and asked God to please hear me, that I needed His strength, His love, to carry me through. I knew I couldn't do it alone. I continued to sob, pleading, to the point where I began to black out, and suddenly, out of nowhere, I felt the most amazing sense of love and peace come over my body. I had never felt something so strong. The feeling spread throughout my entire being, so that suddenly, I was completely calm. I lay there, clutching a shirt to my face, so my children wouldn't hear me, and I felt my whole body become warm. I was calm. I was comforted. I was at peace.

From that moment, I knew I was not alone in my life, and in this process. I knew I was not going to overcome my battle alone. I knew right then and there, that I would choose to stand up for my children, for myself, and for what was right and good. I made a commitment to focus on building a new life for my family, an amazing life, and I would never go back to feeling the way I had. I knew it would take time, and incredible amounts of physical and emotional strength, but at that point, there was no question in my mind of whether I could do it. I knew I could, and I would. I made the choice for a better life, I committed to myself, and I never looked back.

The journey from then on was amazing. I began intense therapy to reprogram my brain, and to undo the conditions I had been led to believe were normal, for so many years. The process was not easy. I had to let go of the anger, the resentment. I had to be completely honest with myself and where I was, so I could learn how to fix it. I had to forgive myself for allowing my children and me to be in that situation. I knew the road ahead would be beyond difficult.

Something happens to you when you start to break free. You ignite a spark, which you've never felt before. And this spark proves that you can overcome your worst fears, your obstacles, your mountains. Each time you push yourself to do this, the spark continues to grow, until it becomes a full flame burning inside of you, pushing you through everything standing in your way.

I told myself I would never again allow anyone to control my identity, my self-worth, or allow me to feel insecure. I would never depend on another's opinion of me for validation, or my happiness. Happiness is a state of mind; it's a choice, a journey. You choose happiness. You create it. Way too many people become dependent upon external things to determine their happiness, and completely underestimate the power of the mind.

What do you tell yourself, every day? Are you sabotaging your success with negative self talk? During this process, when I found a negative thought entering my mind, I immediately replaced it with a positive. This was not always easy. Sometimes it was something as simple as a small, beautiful flower, or the blue sky; that was my positive. It was not a day-to-day process. Sometimes it was focusing enough to get through the next hour.

When you learn how to control your thoughts, you possess power over everything that happens to you. You don't allow external forces and issues to control your emotions; you are in control. Becoming a master of yourself is a constant process. As the negatives continued to come, I dealt with them as needed, and left them behind me. I studied and learned more about the power of the subconscious mind, about the power of mindset, and truly learned how to become a master of myself. I was no longer affected by other's words, or manipulation tactics. I was no longer controlled by fear. I learned how to separate love and control, to love unconditionally, without any expectations. I let go of the anger, the resentment. I began to know me. I didn't just need to become the woman and mother my children needed, I wanted to become her, for myself.

I wanted to become the woman who didn't need validation from anyone. The woman who knew her self worth, who was confident, yet humble, who lived by gratitude, service, and love for God and others. I wanted my children to have a mother they could believe in, and who would be an example in their lives, who embraced life every single day, because of the simple beauties found inside of our world. I wanted my children to have a mother they could be proud of, and look up to. I wanted them to know, that no matter what cards you are dealt, no matter which situation or circumstance you are in, you always have the option to choose otherwise.

As I look back through the years, I am completely amazed by what I have been able to accomplish. There are times when I had no idea how I was able to push through, and it's during those times that I know I was carried. I know I was put on this earth to do more, be more, and I chose that path. I chose to stand up for myself, to love myself, but not just for myself. I chose that path to become an example to others. To become a shining light for them, when they felt they had none. If I can inspire others to believe in themselves, to love themselves, to be confident in who they can become, regardless of their situation or circumstance, then my life has been a success.

To me, success is not the shiny things. It's not the big house on the hill, but something different. It's seeing my children grow into amazing adults. It's being in a position financially to have the freedom and flexibility to help others. It's having an impact on someone's life for the positive, and being an example of what you can accomplish when you truly put your mind to it. If I can inspire others to break free from abusive situations, to love themselves enough to fight for a better life, then I have succeeded. To personally witness an individual fighting for their dream, overcoming challenges and fears, and believing in themselves, is one of the most amazing things. To be able to feel completely free, alive, happy, empowered, and to know you are in control of your thoughts, actions and behaviors; this to me is true success.

I have never regretted what I went through. I now refuse to allow challenges and obstacles to upset me when they come my way, for these are what make me who I am. I choose to look at every experience as a learning experience. I constantly work to keep my mindset right, and to stay mentally and emotionally strong. I choose to allow every experience to make me stronger and wiser.

Life is what we make of it. Every single one of us is blessed with the opportunity to choose. I chose not to be the victim. I chose life. I chose my family. I chose myself. And as I look today at my life and my children, I am in awe. Never underestimate your true potential. Life is meant to be a beautiful adventure.

Johanna Stock has been involved in different business and franchise ownerships, throughout the years. For the last 10 years, Johanna has been a serial entrepreneur. Five years ago she transitioned full-time into the financial industry, where she immediately became passionate about educating people in finance, and empowering others to learn how to take control of their own lives. She is currently licensed in several different states, and works with clientele around the country.

Johanna has four beautiful children, and is currently a mentor, leader, and licensed wealth partner with Elite Hathaway. In her free time, Johanna loves to volunteer, keep herself fit through martial arts, and of course, spend time with her family and friends; knowing the importance of balancing home life, as well as a business.

Today, Johanna teaches women, clients, and organizations across the U.S. the importance of money and self-development. She is a public speaker and, she leads programs to help achieve financial independence and conscious happiness.

To all my dear friends: please text GIFT to
(385) 404-8720 to receive a $998.00 dollar value Education Consultation Program, completely FREE.
This plan will be a game changer in your financial future.

If you want to find out more about Johanna, email her at
Me@johannastock.com ,
Find her on Instagram @ johanna_stock
And Facebook - Johanna Stock

Glimpse of Absent Connections
By Briana Baptiste

There is a difference between being alone and feeling lonely, and I'm sure you've experienced it too.

Being alone is incredible! You don't have to be influenced by anything around you, or the world! It's your time to do whatever the HELL you want! Personally, I enjoy meditating and raising my vibrations as I listen to music. In addition, you can REALLY enjoy the peace and quiet. Or perhaps it's not so peaceful and quiet, because you want to sing your favorite song, and even if it's terrible, well, there's nobody around. You also have the opportunity to self-reflect, build charisma, and share with other people. Yes, being alone is like a light switch. Being in the presence of others flips the switch.

Feeling lonely is different. You can still be amongst others but feel a sense of emptiness. It's like a void that needs to be filled. Humans need to connect in order to stay sane, in my humble opinion. But also, feeling lonely can be dangerous! It can keep a person in a toxic relationship to prevent that feeling of loneliness. But as long as they are comfortable being alone, they can embrace the temporary loneliness.

When I was a child, my only companions were the many toys my mother purchased. She gave me everything I could possibly ask for, and to this day I appreciate it. She helped shape me into the young woman that I am today. Single parenting is not an easy task, not by a long shot. My mom played both roles well - a tough disciplinarian like a father, and a strong, sweet-natured role as a mother.

Sadly, the only connection I have with my estranged biological father and siblings is our last name. I lived with my dad and siblings for a few days at a time on and off. My memories of a having a great time are slim to none, but I remember the traumatic ones. My half-siblings are older than I am, and did a poor job at staying in touch. That's it! Even in my childhood, my siblings were absent. At such a young age, I couldn't understand why we didn't connect, why I couldn't have a deeper connection with them. I felt like something was wrong with ME! I thought maybe... I'm the youngest one... So, I get left out the most.

As I grew up, so did my resentment along with A LOT of built-up anger. I didn't understand why my siblings didn't take the initiative to keep in contact. And then, during my teenage years, I found out that I had ANOTHER half-sister. I was surprised and saddened because once again, another estranged sibling.

Throughout the years, I've watched and admired other families, and I've always analyzed their relationships. Deep down, my heart yearned for a closer bond with my father and siblings. I wanted to connect, bond, and experience the closeness and the love I saw among siblings. Even though it has always appealed to me, it hasn't happened and so, I've moved on.

I grew up with a pattern of seeing people appear and disappear from my life, whether it was through separation or death. In Barbados, there was this beautiful person who I looked forward to seeing each and every time I visited the island. His name was Andre; luckily he was adopted into our awesome family as a baby. He turned out to be the best uncle I could ask for in my ENTIRE life. To me he was more of a brother. He always took good care of my cousin and I, and he was fun-loving and encouraging. He left memorable moments behind. He's someone I looked up to because he was high-energy, loyal, funny, and carried a vibrant smile. My heart carries fond memories of Andre and our beloved connection. Unfortunately, my dear Andre passed away from a heart attack which left me in an utter state of sadness and disbelief, and once again, I felt that sense of loss.

But, instead of being jealous or even envious of others, I decided from a tender age that I would embark on a lifelong journey to connect with people from all over the world and to form lifelong bonds, friendships, and relationships.

As a child, I had an empty feeling, which lasted, throughout my school years. Seeing other classmates with their siblings always reminded me of what I didn't have. In pre-Kindergarten, I met a beautiful and jovial soul named Emily. Looking at photographs of us playing and smiling helped me to recall our memorable moments. Emily definitely fulfilled the feeling that I yearned for; connection.

Then, I switched schools and my friendship with Emily was lost. It was then that I experienced losing someone dear to me. When you're that young, you don't understand the world around you. Things just happen; life goes on! And I didn't grasp this concept yet. Abby Lee from the television show, *Dance Moms* says, "Everyone is replaceable." And even though Emily was not replaceable, I met another childhood friend named Kim at my new school. But, I switched schools again, and this time, I felt another huge sense of loss and loneliness that I carried on with me.

It wasn't until 3rd grade that I came across someone very different, who later became my best friend, and we developed a sisterhood. She had the blackest hair I'd ever seen, pale skin and a strange and serious looking face. She looked unapproachable, so the other kids stayed at a distance. But as a child, it's so much easier to make friends and we had a great friendship. Her mysterious persona appealed to me; I needed to know more about her character. She was like a crab coming out of its shell. Over the years we had play dates, sleepovers, and hangouts, and we formed a deep bond; an unbreakable one (or so I thought).

Luckily, we shared a wide range of interests while learning new things about ourselves. Some of our favorite pastimes were drawing (animals and basic anime characters) and listening to Japanese pop music. She even introduced me to artists like Takamasa Ishihara (better known as "Miyavi") and watching Miyazaki and anime films. It was around this time that I developed a keen interest in other cultures, specifically the Japanese culture.

When we got a little older we had a major dispute that didn't seem solvable. We went our separate way and we are no longer friends. They say all good things come to an end, but I believe it may never end; it lives on only if you allow it. I have many sacred moments from that friendship that I keep alive.

My mom attended college/university as an adult and I attended numerous classes alongside her, even as a young child. I guess you could say, I attended college even before I knew what it really was. I witnessed her hard work, perseverance, and determination, as well as her ability to stay focused on her studies and work, and take care of me full-time.

At ten years old, while sitting in my mom's classes my thoughts always went elsewhere. I never knew how my life would line up for the future. During my mother's last year of university, she met a quirky, gentle, and wide-smiling Japanese native in her communications class. We were introduced and my fascination and love for the Japanese culture grew even more.

We quickly became best buddies and I immersed myself in learning about her culture, food, family, and language. She also travelled back and forth to Japan and brought us many gifts. My favorite gift was a Kimono. It made me feel like a princess, with the colorful fabric and the way the sleeves draped around me. But then, after her graduation, she moved to another country. Again I'd lost someone dear to me and that deep sense of loss came back. She was like an older sister I've never known but have always wanted. Now, I've matured enough to understand that some people enter our lives to teach us important lessons, share good laughs, make memories, and move on to their next journey.

Throughout the years I've lost connection with many people. Sometimes my life feels like a revolving door. Yet, I've learned how to appreciate each and every person who crossed my path. Some have made me cry, others have made me laugh, and some have even made an impact on my life in a negative and positive way. Overall, I've grown, and most of all I'm grateful. I can't deny that I have issues about letting people in. If they get too close I shy away, because now I have the power to choose what feelings I allow into my life. Loneliness is no longer one of them.

Gratitude is sometimes under-rated, but I choose to be grateful in every aspect of my life. I've learned we're all responsible for creating a positive world. I'm not waiting on other people, including my dad or my siblings, to make me happy.

For those of you who may have experienced some of what I've

shared, learn to surround yourself with people who will influence your creative flow and allow your passions to fire. And lastly, YOU ARE the light source, capable of lighting up the space you're in.

Briana Baptiste is a language enthusiast, avid explorer, and Kibun Goddess!

Briana is a creative Scorpio, who is naturally driven and curious. She embodies many talents and is always thinking of new ways to learn and expand her knowledge about cultures and places.

She is an avid gamer, photographer, musician, model, artist, and blogger. To date, she has competed in and won several Equestrian and Gymnastics competitions.

Briana is a visionary and aspiring entrepreneur. She believes that authentic friendships are created by learning new languages to connect and remove inhibitions. She also has an active blog named Kibun Dimensions.

She currently resides with her mom and grandma with their malicious Maltese, Sexy Lexii.

Contact Briana at kibundimensions@gmail.com and check out her blog at https://kibundimensions.blogspot.com/

Stop Being a Victim and Start Being a Victor!
By Debbie Hart

There it was. That moment that changed everything. The moment you realize your life will never be the same. The one you never imagined, that makes you question every decision you have ever made.

Suddenly I was homeless and penniless, with six children in tow. "How did this happen?" I wondered aloud.

I looked at the divorce papers I had just been served, which included a letter from an attorney stating that I must leave the property immediately or be arrested for trespassing. I would be allowed to come back later to collect my personal items.

I didn't know what to do. I could either fall apart, or I could hold it together and make the best of this terrible situation. Falling apart was not an option in my mind. I had children who needed me. So I helped the kids gather what we could in five minutes, then called someone I had only known for two months to ask if the seven of us could move in.

How easy it would have been to fall to pieces! But I committed to myself that day that I would not become bitter. That was a battle, I still had to face.

Ten years prior, I had fallen apart in a different way. I got married right after high school and had my first four children in the space of just five years. I loved my family, but I hurt so much inside. My husband worked long hours and rarely came home, so my days and nights were full of diapers and dishes, fulfilling the endless needs of many small children, and nothing else. I became sick, fatigued, and overweight.

I ran across a small book for losing weight with self-hypnosis. I knew I had nothing to lose (but weight!) and tried it. I quickly noticed incredible results! This began my journey of realizing I could change the results that I experience in life; that I didn't have to just keep allowing life to happen TO me, but that things could start to happen FROM me!

That was the beginning of freedom for me. I started studying personal development and began to change my life. I learned how to have natural childbirths, and I felt so empowered I taught other women and nurses how to do the same. I began acting with a local theater, then started teaching a children's performing group of my own. I started a community theater. I went to trade schools all over, getting certifications in different courses. I formed my own position inside a wellness center and helped clients transform their own struggles. I built a life I loved, instead of enduring the hand that was dealt to me.

Unfortunately, my spouse did not share my new love of life. He undermined my progress at every turn. He called my boss to have me fired. Later, when I brought him into the community theater hoping that he would find the joy I experienced, he instead began tearing me down. I could never understand why. Not only did it cause heartache to hear my own husband speak unkindly about me instead of proclaiming his love for me, but most of the things he said were absurd and untrue! I now understand that angry people often only feel better by hurting others, even when they know what they are doing and saying is false.

But I buried my head in the sand thinking that if I was just kind and forgiving, or just kept enduring, things would get better. They didn't. They got worse! So as shocked as I was at the way my husband left, I shouldn't have been surprised. There were red flags all along the way.

There was a time in this journey where the darkness overcame me. I gave into the pain and fear. I felt justified in doing so, bouncing around in other people's basements with my children and no income for months. I endured threats against me that if I didn't sign away most of my financial rights, my ex would sue for custody. The fear that I could really lose my children bore into me because I was homeless and unemployed. Of course, it was my spouse that had caused both of those things to happen in the first place!

But when I focused on the pain and loss, the stress took a toll. I lost so much weight I could pull on size-zero jeans without unbuttoning them. My hair fell out. I experienced chest pains and even breathing became difficult at times.

I wanted to get back to who I had been. But I couldn't. She was gone. Life would never be the same. I would never be the same. I had to allow myself time to grieve the loss of the life I thought I was going to live.

It was time to create something new. But what? And more importantly how? Through trial and error, while holding intentional space, I became someone who was more capable and stronger than she ever imagined she could be before the split.

Healing began with gratitude. There is good in everything that happens if you are willing to look for it. I first focused on what I learned from each family we lived with. I felt gratitude for their charity. And I discovered new skills for our family.

Next, I worked on forgiveness. Everything works together for our good, even the hard stuff. But only if we let it. The only way I could truly move forward was to let go of the past. Whatever we focus on expands. If we focus on the past, we stay stuck there. So, one day I told my story for the last time, and from then on, I spent the rest of my time and energy creating a new story.

The next step was to eliminate my lone-wolf syndrome. In those early weeks, I remember people offering to help, but I would say, "We are fine." I quickly realized my children and I were not fine. I did need help. We are never meant to go through life alone and it's okay to say 'yes' to help. I always preferred to be the giver before this time. It feels good to be the one who can give, rather than the one who needs help. But how can anyone give if no one is willing to receive? I got into a space of allowing others to help us get back on our feet, and we grew closer in love and unity through that beautiful process.

The thing that helped me heal and transform the most was inner work. It was time for me to look within and take ownership for my part. Although it feels easier to blame others, the blame game only keeps us stuck. If you want something different you need to do something different. For things to improve, you must improve!

Although I had created a life I loved, it obviously did not spill over onto my marriage relationship. That area got worse. So, I dove into my self-discovery process. What was my part in the dissolved marriage? What could I learn? How could I do better next time? It can be painful to look in yourself this way. But it's the only way to create lasting change. Insanity is doing the same thing and expecting different results. The only way for our outer world to change is by working on ourselves.

At first, I was outward focused. I was consumed and baffled by my ex's behavior, so a counselor gave me a book called, *Why Does He Do That? Inside the Minds of Angry and Controlling Men,* by Lundy Bancroft. The book provided relief and understanding around what seemed like craziness to me, and explained the lies at every turn, but it did little to improve my situation at the time. *Respect-Me Rules*, by Michael J. Marshall and Shelly Marshall, helped me understand how my "give in to get along" mentality taught my husband how to treat me poorly. This book helped me discover ways I had not defended myself, and how that only made the behavior escalate over time. Reading from experts and having professional support is key to moving forward in life!

Finally, I needed direction. I knew I wanted to continue in the personal-development field because it lights my soul on fire! I also knew a key ingredient was mastering relationships, because much of our underlying success in other areas of our lives is directly affected by our relationships! If our relationships are going well, we have drive and energy to do well in other areas. The reverse is also true! I went to school again and added relationship coaching to my repertoire. As I enjoyed improved relationships in my personal life, I felt better all around and so did my clients.

With the right tools, you can get through any challenge. Look for the good and express gratitude daily. Let go of grudges so you can stop living in the past. Surround yourself with supportive people who love you and will encourage you. And be willing to look within for what you can improve, committing daily to work toward your goals! Get clear on what you want. With purpose and direction, life can happen FROM you, instead of TO you! Experience more meaning, purpose, and joy in your life. If I can do this, YOU can do this too!

Debbie Hart is an advanced life and relationship coach. From her office in Provo, Utah, she offers Skype and phone sessions around the world! She has successfully worked with many couples in creating a marriage of deep connection, passionate love, and fierce commitment.

Debbie has worked with hundreds of men, women, teens, and children to help them break free of challenges holding them back in many different areas of their lives, from stress management, to breaking bad habits, to starting their own business. She also coaches people on personal development, emotional mastery, life purpose, goal achievement, creative income, and entrepreneurship. She has an advanced specialty in relationships. Her processes combine achievement, inner work, somatic experiences, and relationship coaching for a holistic approach to living a life you love on every level.

When not helping others improve their lives, she spends time with her children playing, hiking, exploring, traveling, painting, and singing. She has additional books and CD's coming out this year. You can discover more at www.PhoenixHigherLiving.com

Follow Phoenix Higher Living on Facebook and Instagram for more!
https://m.facebook.com/PhoenixHigherLiving/
Instagram: Debbie_Hart_

Debbie leaves 2 spaces each week for new client complimentary strategy sessions. Send an email to Debbie@PhoenixHigherLiving.com for availability or click the "Book Now" button right from the website!

The Animals Are Your Clients
By Kim Maksym

Like Dorothy from the *"Wizard of Oz"*, my spiritual journey of truth and empowerment, began with Toto, red slippers, and the yellow brick road.

"The animals are your clients and they will bring you their people." St. Francis of Assisi gave me these exact words many rainbows ago.

At a workshop, to create and market events, I struggled with who I would serve first - adults, children, or dogs. As a Holistic Nutritionist, I was passionate about growing up puppies and babies to live their healthiest, happiest lives. At break-time, a classmate, Frances, who didn't know my quandary, privately gave me this message from St. Francis: *"The animals are your clients."*

St. Francis of Assisi is my Patron Saint, my Glinda, so he did not surprise me, but his message did. My current clients were people. If they had an animal companion, I often helped them too.

That afternoon, conflicted by St. Francis' message, I felt I'd be abandoning the people I helped. Shortly after that, Frances, a gifted reader, conveyed another message from St. Francis. *"The animals will bring you their people."*

I traveled many miles on my yellow brick road through the magical land of Oz, yet I still had more to learn for myself.

The cyclone, that abruptly changed my life, struck when I was seven. My mother and I were traumatized when two men broke into our house one night. Less than two years later, my father, who was only twenty-nine years old, died. My mother, just twenty-five, and alone with four children to raise, died emotionally with him. Imminently, my stepfather joined us; both he and my mother drowned their problems with alcohol. Children of alcoholics do not really grow up in a "family." We were separate individuals, living under one roof.

I grew up in an unprotected environment. Moving numerous times, and rarely finishing a full year at any school, it was difficult to maintain friendships. Though I was sexually abused, I have no memory of who they were, nor does it matter. What I vividly remember is, I disconnected from my body and encountered angels every time - two guardian angels on either side of me, and seraphim angels above me.

This was the perfect childhood for my best friends to be animals, because I learned people were untrustworthy. At a very early age, I could sense animals' souls and compassionately connected with them. Animals loved me unconditionally. People did not. Billy and Bobby were my calf companions, on my grandparent's farm. Once they grew up, I traumatically learned where meat came from. In a meat-eating family, I vowed never to eat animals. The thought of eating my friends was horrific. I knew I did not *need* to eat animals and decided, in childhood, to become a vegetarian, proving it would be my life study.

Marriage, six children, stay-at-home mom, country-living, vegetarianism, home-schooling, church-going, teaching community nutrition classes ... This merry time in the enchanted forest led away from the turmoil of my childhood.

All memories of my first 18 years were blocked. Recently, I began remembering what I need to know. But while raising my children, unknown fears surfaced. Emotional fear wearied my body. I became ill with Chronic Fatigue Syndrome, Multiple Sclerosis, and Lupus. By my late thirties, I lay twenty-two hours in bed daily, and needed assistance to walk. Doctors advised prednisone which would give my life quality, but take quantity. My future looked bleak, and my girlfriends were planning my funeral. I was not. I knew with impeccable certainty, I'd be well. I was drawn to Louise Hay's book, *Heal Your Life,* and counseling.

I always knew bodies could heal themselves with nature's nutrients. The specific nutrients took me three years to find. Then I worked on emotional, spiritual, and physical aspects, and seven months later I was completely well. The gift of dis-ease (lack of ease or disharmony) was that I was healed of major illnesses, so I expanded into becoming a Holistic Nutritionist and Wellness Coach, and I had a supplement line to share with my clients.

Then the Wicked Witch of circumstance flew into my life, ruining my marriage, inflicting tragedies upon my children and animals, and forcing me to leave structured religion.

But the Poppy Field soothed my soul and loved my heart back to a strong beat. I surrendered each challenge, and with light-weight slippers upon my feet, I waltzed towards the Emerald City.

Dancing along my yellow brick road, I received a call from a school-girl who knew I helped animals. She fostered a guide dog named Paige, who had trained for a year to assist a handicapped person. Paige pushed elevator buttons, rode escalators, and retrieved items. At the time of her sale and placement, she became gravely ill with Hemophiliac Anemia. Unwell with her ongoing treatment of medications, blood transfusions, urine and blood tests, the society decided to put Paige to sleep, despite her training, and huge monetary value. When asked if I could help her, I immediately said, "Yes." The Society donated Paige to me. I instantly felt her illness in my own body, and became ill like her. I knew intuitively what she needed - body, mind, and spirit. Within three weeks, she was fully well and off all treatment. One of the major components of her healing was that I put Paige on a vegetarian diet.

"You are more capable than you know."

I am an empath but never understood the depth, until Paige. Her heart's desire was to stay with me, and the Society never asked for her back.

My veterinarian, who monitored Paige's miraculous progress, encouraged me to write Paige's story and a vegetarian cookbook for dogs. Fear held me back. When I heard other authorities say dogs required meat, I doubted myself, believing they were the wizards, and I stayed small.

I walked many bricks before I attended the workshop in 2010, where I received St. Francis' message. But even after the workshop, I continued working with people. I couldn't envision my services differently.

People with serious illnesses came. I loved helping them; however, this took much energy out of me. Between clients, there was always a recharge time of up to two weeks. During one period of exhaustion, St. Francis told me directly, if I continued to lead with people, I would wear myself out and die.

"You've always had the power; you just had to learn it for yourself."

Instantly, I realized I was exhausted because I was not fully aligned with my soul's truth, and only I had the power to change that.

The animals are the ones I must help, and they will bring me their people, not the other way around. I had searched everywhere outside of me, when this truth was always within.

"If I ever go looking for my heart's desire again, I won't look any further than my own backyard. Because if it isn't there, I never really lost it to begin with."

I clicked my heels three times, proclaiming *"There is no place like home."* Once I embraced my truth, I was finally home-sweet-home in my heart.

Over-the-rainbow excited to change my business, I wondered how the animals would find me. St. Francis told me Paige and the Fairies would guide them to me.

The next day, I began feeling a dog's Colitis, aware it was not mine. Three days later her person called me. Working with them both, I found the dog had the physical symptoms and her person had the emotional symptoms. I knew how to help both. I have felt many ailments since. As St. Francis told me, the people would come to me through the animals; the animals and fairies do guide their people to contact me by email or telephone. Paige and I are a team. She is a wise, gentle teacher, and crystal dog – my Toto. Animals and children, who come to us, are sensitive. Paige loves and welcomes everyone. In our home, she calms dogs with anxiety. She helps potty train; I've heard her tell puppies "Go to the bathroom, and then we'll play."

I love making a difference for animals and their families, relating their animal's wisdom, feelings, and information. Their messages may include what they're helping their people with, what they wish to eat, their will to live, if they want another companion, or how they feel about their name.

It breaks my heart to feel a dog's crushed spirit because he doesn't feel he has purpose, feels misunderstood, depressed, lonely, bored, in pain, or has a health challenge there are answers for. It saddens me deeply when animals have little appetite and are bored with their food. Like us, animals have taste buds and what one dog may like, another may be repulsed by, much like my distaste for the headcheese my step-father forced us to eat as children.

My heart goes out to children having difficulty concentrating at school because they don't have the nutrition to nourish their brain, or when parents don't know how to feed their children, let alone their dog. It's my greatest pleasure to help families plan simple meals all beings will enjoy.

"It's not where you go. It's who you meet along the way."

My life's work has been a process of discovery and of reflection. Each challenge has held within it a greater lesson and gift to bring to the world. I could not have planned this journey, even if I had wanted to. And I wouldn't have come back Home, if I hadn't walked through the dark forests and along the long and tiring yellow brick road. I am grateful for every person and animal I met along the way, my sparkling, red slippers, and always having a faithful companion by my side.

Often called the *Fairy Best DogMother*, Kim Maksym and her Therapy Dog Paige, help dogs and their people live their best lives. As a Holistic Nutritionist, Coach, Wellness Intuitive and Energy Therapist, her work encompasses body, mind, and spirit. She focuses on the connection and purpose between animals and their human companions, and provides caregiving for dogs in her loving home. Kim loves and honors all of God's creatures, is a mother and grandmother of six, and has cared for 33 animals throughout her journey. If you visit her acreage, you may find her petting bumblebees outside in the summer, or in her home feeding ladybugs in the winter.

Kim's hobbies include ballroom dancing, gardening, and spending time with her animal companions. She writes a weekly newsletter for the Edmonton dance community.

Kim studied with the Cosmetology School of Canada, CUC, Weimar Institute, Proevity, and the Global College of Natural Medicine.

You may contact Kim or find out more about her services at www.kimmaksym.com; www.thefairybestdogmother.com; or "The Fairy Best DogMother" on facebook

For 50% off a session with Kim for your animal companion, please email Kim at thefairybestdogmother@gmail.com with "Courageous World Catalysts 50% Discount" in the subject line.

Envision
By Sharon Kambale

I remember like it was yesterday. A grey Friday morning in August, 2011. I woke up in a state of agony. I knew it was time. The birth of my first born was just moments away. As we made our way towards the NICU, my mom walked with solidified strength. She showed strength I needed to push forward into the next stage of life. Upon the arrival of what we had long waited for, I was quickly filled with excitement. She was a perfect little girl! Ten fingers, ten toes, and a cute button nose. A gift from above. I held her in my arms, and at the moment our eyes locked, I was granted renewed purpose. Even though I was scared, she helped me know that everything would be okay. I gazed up and asked, "What should I name her?" Mom proudly replied, "Flavia, after your aunt." Though life had handed me many challenges, I was sure about one thing, together, Flavia and I were called for so much more. Lady Via was born.

Some of the challenges I experienced were false romances and financial instability. After Flavia's birth, we lived in government housing and relied upon social welfare. We lived in one of the worst neighbourhoods called Dover in the city of Calgary, Alberta. Dover was known for its drugs and crime epidemic, the darkness of poverty.

I greatly believed if I only spoke of the good, then only good would happen. I would remain un-judged and safe and life would be okay. I simply just needed to maintain the image I presented. No one would need to know my reality -- that I depended on government hand-outs. It was at this time that I began to envision a different life. I envisioned leaving behind a life filled with false relationships with men who lied between their teeth. I envisioned that I would settle down and finish university. I was determined to break a cycle so entrenched within the history of my family. And so I began to feel displaced in my circumstances. I longed for a place of belonging where truth was one of acceptance.

I often questioned how a woman would ever stay in an abusive relationship. Until it was me. I hoped that things will get better; that

I would be able to move from the four walls I had caged myself in and be able to face the world. I hoped to heal and move forward, to leave behind the curse that was rooted within. I often wondered whether I would wake up from this nightmare and be able to turn back time, to a time of purity and innocence, back to my childhood.

As a five-year-old, I was described as vibrant and determined. I remember an active childhood filled with great imagination. Involved in music and sports, I innately was drawn to helping others at every opportunity I was given. It was in my early years that I began to lead. I felt a sense of compassion for those in need. Despite growing up in two homes separated by divorce, I was always encouraged to place faith and education at the forefront of all that I did. However, I was determined to prove my own voice. I began to desire a life of independence where I could pave a way on my own. In my eagerness, I left home at the tender age of 14.

School had always been my safe haven. A home away from home. It provided a sense of belonging and support, which I greatly needed. As a young student I was provided the support and the love that I longed for. I looked up to teachers for guidance as they met my needs. One time, in grade two, a teacher provided my siblings and me winter boots. There were also the times I was fed food from the school pantry. It was during these moments when I yearned for financial freedom. By participating in the extra-curricular activities there was a sense of belonging and acceptance. Collectively we could relate. After-school programs also provided an opportunity to be creative, a value that has helped me attain a dynamic perspective on life.

At a young age I sought attention, which often meant destructive behaviors. I acted out, dated around, and whatever trouble I could find, I did. But there were things I still loved about school. I remember the school dances. But most importantly I remember spending hours and hours reading. I read novels upon novels because they took me to a magical place far away from my unhappy world. Books changed my life in ways that I never thought they would. They brought answers to my questions. Often they were books about girls who broke free from hurt and became something in their world. I began to realize I could too. I began to understand that my past did not have to be my future.

I started to be more optimistic and became involved in church. I joined the worship team which provided the space to express my voice through music. Church reminded me that I was loved. I made it a point to attend youth nights and began to journal every day. My journals would start, "Dear Heavenly Father, thank you so much for…." as I felt protected by something larger and greater than myself. An earthly angel would always be within arm's reach to ensure that I was on the right path. Someone to protect me from danger. Someone heaven sent.

I began to rise above obstacles and achieve increased success. At age 16 I purchased my first car, a standard, and my independent accommodation. At age 21 I opened a space to empower females so that they too could gain clarity, which was later showcased on national TV. They say "age is just a number." It really is. You can be whatever you want, have whatever you want. As long as you believe in YOU no one can stand in your way.

After the birth of Flavia I continued to envision. I envisioned being the leader I was called to be. I began to face the fears I so deeply dreaded. I began to take action. I enrolled myself in community college and became active within church. Every Sunday during the service I would ask God for continued strength and the ability to move forward and to be an example for others. You see, it was here that I reinvented the stories that I had been trapped in. No longer would I continue the path of disruption, but rather Flavia and I would begin to accept the purpose that stood before us.

As a mother I was seen as an example. I was seen as a leader. I was able to lead others to also take action towards their purpose. I continued to bridge the difference between two worlds so greatly divided.

This bridge is about the process of forgiveness; forgiving those who have brought pain and choosing to switch your life story. I understood that I needed to take responsibility and define my story. It was about the ability to forgive myself and others and to learn from my mistakes. Most importantly it was about surrendering to

God and fully accepting Him into my life. Through self-awareness and self-acceptance, I started to unleash myself from the poison of hatred I had carried for too long. As I blossomed, curiosity flowed.

Upon completing community college in the Summer of 2013, I took it upon myself to travel to Entebbe, in Kampala, Uganda, a trip without a plan but with a purpose. I would serve God in the way in which I was called. I had always dreamed of going back home to Entebbe since the time I was a child. Mom always reminded us of how life back home was vastly different from what we knew in the West.

As I stepped off the plane and into the airport I truly began to understand how fortunate I was to have the life I was granted. Poverty was evident. During my trip I gained so much. I gained first-hand experience of how Uganda is stripped of its natural resources, and is thus subject to social, economic, and political instability. However, poverty does not stop love. The heart of the people was so real. During my trip I could see how the culture of music brought people together, something so simple and inexpensive. If people could be so happy with so little, then it was evident that change came from within. My commitment to be a world changer was deepened. It was through this trip that I gained further acceptance of where I had been, who I was, and where I was going.

Upon arriving back in Calgary, I began to take further steps into the purpose Flavia and I were destined for. I was accepted into the university in Saskatoon, Saskatchewan. During my time at the university I came to understand what it meant to be an authentic leader. In 2014, I became an academic mentor to support those who were also looking to attain clarity for their future. I was re-elected as the representative for Social Work students through the University of Regina. I also got married, and we now have our youngest Françia who has also taught us so much. I have been featured on CTV National, have coached several people closer to their truths, and have been fortunate enough to visit London to meet beautiful, like-minded women.

I am grateful. Not because I have reached my ultimate destination or because I have it all. I am grateful because I am reminded that

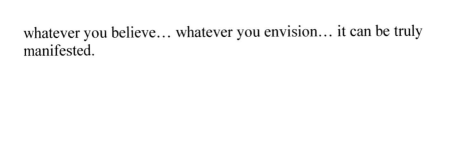

whatever you believe… whatever you envision… it can be truly manifested.

Sharon Kambal is a Holistic Guru, Change Agent, Business and Marketing Strategist with 10-years of experience. She has a feminist criminology background from the University of Saskatchewan, and a social work background from the University of Regina. Sharon has made it her mission to reach out to like-minded queens all across the globe with her message. She feels blessed to have the honor of guiding young women in achieving an authentic lifestyle through her biz, Lady Via: the sisterhood where you are granted the opportunity to achieve your full awesomeness!

Email Sharon at ladyvia@outlook.com and join her Facebook Group Lady Via Monetary Mindset at https://www.facebook.com/groups/385987358444049/

Life in a Heartbeat
By Melinda Maxwell Smith

"Hi, Gram, I'm here. It's Melinda," I hold the soles of her feet through the warmed-up post-op sheet. "Your bypass was a success. You did great! I'll be here while you wake up." I trust she can hear me, even though there's no response, just as I trusted that my newborn babes could hear and understand me. I can see the monitor above her bed. Rounded, loopy tracings of her heart's activity reassure me.

Soft snores come from her dry mouth. I catch a nurse walking by the recovery room and ask for a glycerin swab. In a few minutes she returns with one. The wrapper crackles as I remove the small sponge on a pliable stick. From the side of her bed now, my hands are off her. I see the heart monitor go wacky, jumping, spiking high and low. I put my free hand over hers, and look up. The heart beat gets smoother. "Hmm…" I muse. "Her face went from strained to serene in a heartbeat."

"Here ya go, Gram, I'm going to wet your whistle with some lemony flavored stuff." Her teeth clamp down on the swab and her eyes flutter a bit.

"You're *strong*! You'll be outa here in no time, Gram." Minutes go by. "Ya know… You were caught doing the right thing… *again.* " I squeeze her hand still holding the swab with my other. "What're we going to do with you? Tsk, tsk. You're always doing the right thing. Mmm hmm. Yes, you are." The heart monitor shows smoother, more regular beats, slowing down. "You listened to your body. When it said, 'I need help,' you chose the right doctor to help you. He's good. Now you've got brand new pipes bringing nourishment to your sweet heart."

I press her hand then squeeze her shoulder, avoiding the IV in the crook of her elbow. I look up, surprised my eyes are swimming. It's hard to see the monitor. I release my hand and wipe my eyes with my back-pocket hanky. I look up again. Her heart beat is erratic. Wild. I hold her hand again. Heart beat becomes regular. *Curious.* I wiggle the stick of the mouth swab. She's not letting go.

Slight cough. She releases her bite. Quickly, I swab everything I can reach inside her cheeks and lips. Moisture. My Gram has always loved water. Living a couple of miles from Santa Monica Beach, she often stops in the course of her tasks each day to put her hand over her heart and sniff appreciatively. "Oh, can you smell *that*? That's the *water*. Aren't we lucky?! Don't you just love the moisture?!"

My grandmother Florence was born in England. Her parents moved with their nine children to New York, near the Hudson River, where her father worked as a stone mason on Croton Dam and several houses near Tarrytown. Grammy was the youngest. So many changes she's seen in the world since 1894. I'm glad she lived through all her life's challenges thus far. She saved *my* butt so many times in my thirty-seven years. My eyes are leaky again. I feel love pouring from my grateful heart, into her, as if willing her to get up and walk with me back to her house in Culver City, the most nurturing home I've ever known. I want to be *there* with her and Gramps. *Now*.

The clock reads 5:04. Gramps will have heated the supper I brought for him before coming to the hospital. He starts dinner right at 5:00, like clockwork. Reliable. Comforting. The antidote to the chaos of my childhood home, where my dad was so scary when he was drinking. Daily.

Grammy's eyes flutter again, then shut. Waking up from anesthetic reminds me of birth contractions. She rouses. She rests. Little spurts of wakefulness last longer and come closer together. Still, it might be awhile. I'm glad another carpool mom is picking up my daughters today. My husband will bring them home after work. Our girls love and watch out for each other.

Grammy turns her head ever so slightly. It sounds as if she's trying to clear her throat. Soft groan. "That's right, Gram. Things are going to feel different. Your body is already healing, but it's been through a lot. That was some work-out they gave you… like running a marathon. Pretty good for ninety-one, Gram. *Very* good!"

* * * * * * * * *

Because of the surgery, Grammy lived another six years. At ninety-seven, she was ready to dance with Gramps again. He died just eighteen months before she took her final breath. He was one hundred-years-old when I watched him leave his body.

Our dance that day in the recovery room in 1983, after her triple bypass surgery, is what sent me on my thirty-five year exploration of how humans heal. Surely, it was more than love for my dear Gram that calmed and regulated her heartbeat. I've studied and been certified in so many modalities, I ran out of wall space. I keep the certificates in a binder. Using many different bodywork approaches I've immersed myself in over the years, I support my clients' healing. They come from all walks and all ages. In 1985, I enrolled in Massage School, just to legitimize putting hands on people. I kept studying whatever seemed like my next step for healing myself.

Most of my life, I was tense; afraid to make mistakes, and fearful of being seen, heard, found imperfect, and of being intimate. Being invisible felt safer. My middle name was, "What?" No one could hear me. My closet kept me mostly safe from my father's erratic and dangerous behavior. When I got older, I ran wild through the hills of Echo Park near downtown Los Angeles. I'm just glad I survived my adolescent acting out. Sex, drugs, alcohol, and Rock 'n' Roll got me through the sixties.

At forty-two, married, with two children, memories of early childhood sexual abuse arose. A friend I've known since we were three came to live with my family and me while she and her nearly four-year-old daughter extricated themselves from the child's molesting father. I couldn't understand why I felt nauseous in the little one's presence. I began waking up at night, gagging, unable to breathe, pains in my body, and smelling odors that weren't in the room. I thought I was crazy, thought I was in somebody else's movie. I thought, "This is *really* weird."

My husband and I had just entered couple's therapy. We each had our own therapist. So there was a huge safety net to catch me as I began to unravel what happened to me from a time before I had teeth, until my parents divorced when I was nine years old. When Dad died, I was sixteen. Still, I had no memory of what had happened to me. The trigger of my friend's arrival, and the safety I felt within my created family, allowed the pieces of the puzzle to come into view. I broke secrecy and learned how to compost the incest. The garbage of abuse transformed into rich soil. Some flowers have grown from it, including many songs which I've written and recorded. I vowed to turn poison into nectar so as not to pass down to my children what happened to me.

"What doesn't kill us makes us stronger," said Ernest Hemingway. Now, in my sixties, I'm glad I lived. There were times I seemed hell-bent on killing myself; times I wish I *had* suffocated at the hands of my father's inappropriate use of my body, or died some other way. My perspective from this side of the journey toward wholeness is that it's worth the wild ride. I'm lucky to have survived and to have become a trauma specialist, privileged to witness client's heroic journeys.

"If you're going through Hell, keep going," Winston Churchill said. Clients come to therapy with what Anngwyn St. Just calls 'terrible knowledge.' Whether it's surgery, accidents, falls, abuse, war, gang violence, or birth trauma, within the safety of the therapeutic relationship, the human nervous system knows what to do; how to heal. As babies, we first learn to co-regulate with a stable nervous system (usually our mother's). So, too, is it in body therapy. We learn to co-regulate with our therapist, if s/he has a regulated nervous system, and later to self-regulate. It has been my honor to work with newborns to nonagenarians who have been roughed up by life. I'm never bored. Since moving from Los Angeles to Oakland in late 2014, I've been finding more time to write about the healing I've been privileged to witness.

Thank you, Grammy Florence for holding me in the light.

"The deeper we dare into darkness, the more we're given true sight."
—Melinda Maxwell-Smith

A recent transplant from Los Angeles, Melinda Maxwell-Smith is a native of the hills of Echo Park. Though most of the foxtails have been picked out of her socks, the magic of those hills still lives in her blood. A grateful mother of two accomplished daughters, she now enjoys the hills of Oakland where she and her husband of forty-five years moved to be hands-on grandparents.

Melinda has been writing since she could hold a pencil. Her first tome at age seven was made of recycled Christmas cards. *The Littlest Angle* featured her unintentionally creative alternative spellings. A bodyworker for nearly thirty-five years, specializing in trauma resolution, and a yoga teacher for almost as long, she loves making new friends, making music, and making a difference. She maintains a blog on Birth, Death, and the Stuff in Between.

http://mymondaymuse.blogspot.com/

Waiting to Get Hit by an Eighteen-Wheeler to Finally Live
By Elizabeth de Moraes, M.A, M.F.A.

The crash:
It was the day that everything changed for me.
A busy Dallas highway at rush hour…
A little yellow sports car driving the speed limit with no distractions…
And then, all hell broke loose…

An 18-wheeler behind me tried changing lanes, but didn't see me. She hit me on the back driver's side putting me in a tailspin that could have taken my life. I began spinning in a full circle, which caused me to spin 90° into the truck in front of her. The next thing I saw out my door window was a huge truck driving straight at me at full force.

And BAM! She hit me again, this time shattering the glass onto my seat. My car got dragged sideways until I could break away. I started spinning again, but this time into the next lane on the other side of her. I faced backwards, looking at oncoming traffic, but stuck sideways against the truck. Her wheels tore up the side of my car. I finally was able to break away and started spinning again across another lane. All I could think of at this point was to pray that no other cars would hit me. I finally came to a stop and waited. I waited for someone else to rear end me causing another jolt. I had been hit three times by the semi-truck, spun across three lanes of a busy Dallas highway and no one else hit me. I sat there for a moment, stunned. Was I okay? Was everyone else okay? What do I do now?

After I came to my senses I jumped out of my car on the shoulder, brushed off all of the glass that I was covered in and had been sitting in, and realized I only had one cut in my leg. God and His angels completely guided everything, bringing me gently to a standstill. I was still alive...And for a reason.

The realization:
While spinning, it felt like time stood still with everything in slow

motion, yet simultaneously, it seemed that everything happened so quickly, one after the other after the other. I could hear myself screaming. I felt everything. Every muscle contraction. Every moment. Every thought. Yet I felt completely out of control. All I could think of through this incident was how grateful I was that my two girls weren't with me. After all was said and done, I was simply amazed that I made it through with only one tiny cut on my leg. My cute little yellow sports car was totaled, but I walked away, unscathed.

This was my wake up call.

Throughout my life I felt like I held myself back in so many ways due to a vast array of fears.

Fear of failure.
Fear of success.
Fear of making other people uncomfortable because I strived for a greater life.
Fear of people putting me down while I strived to be my most authentic self.
Fear of looking stupid or not knowing what I thought I should know or should be able to do.

And the list goes on. You get the idea.

For most of my teen and adult years this fear caused me to live a half-life. I so desired success and certain dreams in my life, but before I could even accomplish those things I would stop myself from doing what was necessary to achieve that success, or the income flow, because I felt flawed.

I didn't feel like I was enough. I didn't feel like I was deserving. I felt like something was wrong with me. I felt that I needed to be humble. I felt stupid that I wasn't already "there" (wherever "there" was). I felt guilty for certain things I had done in my life (and they weren't even that bad!). I felt shame as well. How could someone like me, who, felt eternally flawed, allow herself be fully happy and fully expressed in the world? Some of these insecurities might sound familiar in your own life.

These lies I told myself came from the messaging I received throughout my life and my perception of those messages. Those messages created beliefs in me that tainted my experiences and interactions with other people that, in turn, only reinforced those beliefs. It was a vicious cycle.

I self-sabotaged and self-abandoned, so going for that next level of success was terrifying. One of my biggest fears was, and still is to a certain extent, going for that next level of accomplishment and falling flat on my face. Additionally, I was fearful of really going for all my big dreams because I didn't feel I deserved the accolades and the income that would come with such. If I sabotaged the journey in some form or fashion, or limited myself, I wouldn't have to find out or prove to myself that I indeed lacked the talent to reach for the success that I desired to create. Existing this way was a double-edged sword that caused me to live stifled, numb, and paralyzed to what I knew I could truly accomplish in my life.

As an example, I gained weight in my dance career right when I had the opportunity to truly go for that next big audition that would land me a place with my dream dance company. In doing so, I could blame the weight gain, not the potential lack of talent, for not getting to my next big break. There were so many ways that I consciously and unconsciously kept myself from realizing my potential and total joy in life.

Outside, it appeared that I strived successfully and found success. But this impression fostered even more fears that I might seem like a fraud, because I knew that I could be so much more.

And then the crash happened.

Because of the wreck, I realized that I no longer have time to waste playing small in my life and in the world. That huge truck became the symbol of my big life crushing my little life (my small car) once and for all.

God has a big purpose for each of us, and it's our job to fully realize those talents and gifts in the world. I have always known I was meant for great things and could make a big impact. You probably feel the same about yourself. But for years there has always been that "something" holding us back, right?

My friend, it is time to fully step into your greatness. God's greatness. To be the vessel of God's will. It's time to step out of the way of ourselves. We are the only ones holding ourselves back, despite our reasons and excuses for such. This is now my mission: to live and to help others live a fully invested and fully expressed life through personal branding and development of a super-star presence to be shared on video and in business.

The transformation:
One of the most important things we can do in life is to learn from our experiences and, more importantly, act upon them without hesitation. Because of the accident, I am now determined to fully be visible, show up for myself, and to coach others to do the same. I am now fully available to myself and I hope the same for you. We are everything that God created us to be and we deserve every single desire and dream that comes through our soul.

After the accident I took time to really get inside and see the lies I told myself that were so ingrained in every cell of my body and subconscious. I also took time to look at my deepest desires and visions for my life. I let myself dream bigger dreams that felt completely out of reach. The result? Pure amazement at what I could accomplish and what the future holds! Those dreams are actually coming true and I am having a blast!

Because of this shift in mindset, I completely rebranded myself by stepping into the vision that I hold for myself. I let myself believe and act on the belief that by unashamedly and blissfully creating a life and top visual brand that truly represents who I am at the core. I offer the freedom and personal permission for others to do the same.

This is my mission as a company owner, and I am in love with the whole process!

By helping others break their limiting beliefs, they are able to unleash their voices and visual personal brands in a way that is in alignment with who they truly desire to be. This is so that they can be seen as the experts in their industry (and, as a result, make much more money!). It feels fabulous to be able to pull all my talents and skills together from my international professional dance career as a performer, teacher, and choreographer (both on stage and on camera) and transfer that to the entrepreneurial realm and online space. I get to use my creativity, draw from my experiences, and place them in the business world, and it feels freaking awesome! I get to show up as my FULLY expressed self as I help others do the same!

My hope for you is that you don't wait for an 18-wheeler to hit you before you decide that enough is enough. It is completely up to you to make the decision to fully go for your desires in life as every single one is completely possible. Let my story be your wake-up call. Go out into the world and "unleash your own inner celebrity!"™

Elizabeth de Moraes is an International Certified Personal Branding and Video Success Coach. She empowers visionary entrepreneurs who are either their brand, or the spokesperson for their brand, to make more impact and income through connecting with their ideal clients by engaging them in star-quality online videos. From smashing your limiting beliefs around truly being visible to yourself and the world, and support around all the technical elements of video creation, to styling and developing your "it" factor, and on camera delivery, she is your go-to expert!

You are meant to be heard AND seen as an expert and influencer in your industry! It's time to unleash your inner celebrity™!

Get your free social media video creation guide here: https://elidemoraes.lpages.co/theswagbag/

Find out more at www.yourinnercelebrity.com and email Elizabeth at shine@yourinnercelebrity.com

Now that you've read these amazing stories, how would you like to be part of the next anthology project and spread your message worldwide?

All you have to do is turn in your story and I'm going to give you easy-to-follow steps to writing it so that it speaks to those people who need your help. I'm also going to take away the tech overwhelm by publishing the book for you and guaranteeing the Best Seller status. Plus, I'm even going to have your story edited by my team.

➜ Go here for details on the next project – join or get on the waiting list: http://bit.ly/nextanthology

* * * * * * * * * * * * * * *

What's it like being in an athology like this one? Just see what the co-authors of this book say …..

Vickie Gould is absolutely amazing to work with. She has to be the best book coach in the industry by far. For many years, I have had thoughts of being a published author but the thought of writing seemed to be overwhelming. My experience with Vickie has been nothing short of amazing. She has encouraged me to write my message and share it with the world. If you have ever considered publishing your own book or being part of an anthology, please check her out!

~ Sherrod Schuler, MBA Minister, Motivational Speaker and Financial Wellness Coach

It was an easy peasy experience to work under the guidance of Vickie Gould in her Anthology group program. Her coaching, organizational skills, timely emails, her editor, facebook presence, availability whenever I needed her, were all excellent. The program itself was thorough and very well designed. I'm so proud to be a co-author in the Anthology "Courageous World Catalysts".

~ Kim Maksym, The Fairy Best Dogmother

* * * * * * *

Being a co-author in this book, Courageous World Catalysts, has been such an amazing experience and one that I will never forget! It was a pleasure working with Vickie and I am honored and humbled by this whole experience.

It wasn't easy to sit down and write such a personal story. One of the reasons I joined this Anthology was to do just that - tell my story. It was through Vickie's guidance and assurance during this process that afforded me to take a step back and view my story as not one of fear and regret but more of a courageous step knowing that each one of our stories may touch someone in a way where they will stand up and take a courageous action on their own. That's what this Anthology is all about!

From the beginning, Vickie was organized and kept everyone well informed. Her team made this whole process run so efficiently. I look forward to Vickie Gould's next Anthology!

~ Janis Melillo, Wellness/Transformation Health Coach, International Best Selling Co-Author

* * * * * * *

I began working with Vickie Gould by being invited by a friend to be a part of a book project showcasing 36 entrepreneurs and their business. I joined this project because not only did I want to become a published author, but it was in timing of my new business launch. Vickie is a positive, upbeat and empowering woman that makes this process fun. She is very organized, keeps you updated and on task. I would recommend highly recommend working with Vickie. She has a gift in building excitement and motivation.

~ Dawn Laveck-Palfi, Self-Love and Self-Care Advocate/Coach

An opportunity to fulfill a dream is an amazing gift, thank you Vickie Gould for providing me the opportunity to create my dream!

I have had a deep desire to share stories with others with a hope that they can touch a soul and create a path to a happier and more joyful life experience. It is interesting the voices that debate inside the mind. For me, one voice was the voice of encouragement, hope and faith and the second was the antagonist spreading the feelings of doubt, inadequacy and fear. "Write your Stories vs. What are you thinking?

The gift for me was a simple opportunity to take action in an simple way…….Write a simple heartfelt story and trust someone who has the knowledge, skills and experience to place this in a book! Vickie Gould and her team made the dream a reality in a simple process that coached me and the team through this Anthology Book "Courageous World Catalysts"! I will be forever grateful as I now have the courage to move forward and write many more stories and books!

~ Brooks Gibbs, Powerful, Passionate Mirror (Mentor and Coach)

* * * * * * *

Vickie Gould is a powerhouse in supporting your story to be heard and alive in the world! She is a mountain of support - compassionately inspiring the best story out of you! This best selling author knows her stuff from transforming her own life to tell her best selling story to helping others get out of their own way to be able to share their magnificence as well.

~ Kanelli Scalcoyannis, Success Coach & Founder of Luscious Life

* * * * * * *

➔ **Go here for details on the next project** – join or get on the waiting list: http://bit.ly/nextanthology

I can't wait to meet you!